Cycle

TOURS

24 one-day routes in
Gloucestershire and
Hereford & Worcester

Compiled by
Nick Cotton

HAMLYN

Contents

On-road routes

Back cover photograph: Open wold country near Hawling

First published 1993 by

Ordnance Survey   and   Hamlyn, an imprint of
Romsey Road   Reed Books
Maybush   Michelin House
Southampton   81 Fulham Road
SO16 4GU   London SW3 6RB

Text and compilation
Copyright © Reed International Books Ltd 1995
Maps Copyright © Crown Copyright 1995
Second edition 1995

A catalogue record for this atlas is available from the British Library

ISBN 0 600 58665 0
(Ordnance Survey ISBN 0 319 00769 3)

Made, printed and published in Great Britain

Acknowledgements
Nick Cotton *back cover, 19, 31, 37, 91, 107, 111* • Reed International Books (Colin Molyneux) *67, 73* • Judy Todd *85, 97, 119, 123, 131* • Spectrum Colour Library *25, 55, 135*

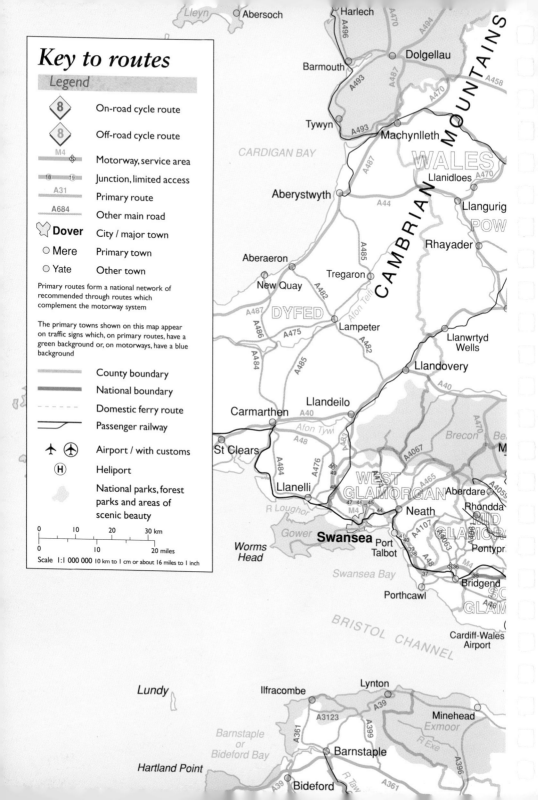

Quick reference chart

Route	Page	Distance (miles)	Grade (easy/moderate/strenuous)	Links with other routes[1]	Tourist information centres[2]
On-road routes					
1 *Leominster to the timber-built villages of Dilwyn, Pembridge and Wigmore*	18	32	✦✦✦✦	2,5	Leominster 01568-616460
2 *East from Leominster to Bromyard*	24	27	✦✦✦	1,3,4	Leominster 01568-616460
3 *From Tenbury Wells to Clifton upon Teme, returning via the Teme Valley*	30	35	✦✦✦✦	2	Leominster 01568-616460
4 *From Ledbury to Bromyard, beneath the Malvern Hills*	36	30	✦✦	2	Ledbury 01531-636147
5 *From Hay-on-Wye to Kington and back via the Wye valley*	42	40	✦✦✦	1,6	Hay-on-Wye 01497-820144
6 *A stiff challenge on the Black Mountains, south of Hay-on-Wye*	48	35	✦✦✦✦✦	5	Hay-on-Wye 01497-820144
7 *North from Ross-on-Wye, following the loops of the River Wye*	54	31	✦✦		Ross-on-Wye 01989-62768
8 *Beneath the Malverns, west of Upton upon Severn*	60	35	✦	9	Upton upon Severn 01684-594200
9 *Dodging the hills east of Tewkesbury*	66	41	✦	8,10	Tewkesbury 01684-295027
10 *The northern Cotswolds, from Stow-on-the-Wold to Moreton-in-Marsh and Chipping Campden*	72	31	✦✦✦	9,11	Stow-on-the-Wold 01451-831082
11 *South from Stow-on-the-Wold to the Windrush Valley and Northleach*	78	31	✦✦✦	10,12	Stow-on-the-Wold 01451-831082
12 *From Cirencester along the edge of the Golden Valley and on to Withington*	84	34	✦✦✦	11	Cirencester 01285-654180
13 *Very easy riding in the Severn Vale around Frampton on Severn*	90	10,12, 12	✦	14	Gloucester 01452-421188
14 *From Wotton-under-Edge to the River Severn, returning via Uley*	96	30	✦✦✦✦	13	Tetbury 01666-503552

[1] **Links with other rides** Use this information to create a more strenuous ride or if you are planning to do more than one ride in a day or on a weekend or over a few days. The rides do not necessarily join: there may be a distance of up to three miles between the closest points. Several rides are in pairs, sharing the same starting point, which may be a good place to base yourself for a weekend.

[2] **Tourist Information Centres** You can contact them for details about accommodation. If they cannot help, there are many books that recommend places to stay. If nothing is listed for the place where you want to stay try phoning the post office or the pub in the village to see if they can suggest somewhere.

Gloucestershire and Hereford & Worcester

Gloucestershire falls easily into three distinct regions: the Cotswolds, the Severn Vale and the Forest of Dean. The Cotswold escarpment runs southwest – northeast from Bath to Chipping Campden and drops sharply to the west towards the Severn Vale. The Cotswolds slope away gently to the east towards Oxford and the Thames. Riding on the top is fairly easy, riding on and off the escarpment fairly strenuous. There are many well-known tourist spots such as Bourton-on-the-Water, Chipping Campden, Stow-on-the-Wold, Moreton-in-Marsh and Broadway but also less frequented villages, linked by delightful quiet lanes. The flat plain created by the River Severn, like the Somerset Levels, provides some of the easiest cycling in Southern England. The Forest of Dean lies to the west of the Severn and forms part of the Welsh Border country. With the exception of a few small areas that are restricted to walkers, there are no limits on the forestry tracks you can use so you can explore at will.

The rolling agricultural landscape and the valleys of the Wye, the Lugg and the Teme form the basis of many of the rides in Hereford and Worcester. Rides start or pass through attractive market towns such as Ross-on-Wye, Bromyard, Ledbury, Leominster and Tenbury Wells, taking in many villages with the black-and-white, half-timbered houses that are so characteristic of the Welsh Marches. Two rides start from Hay-on-Wye, the secondhand book centre of the world, a small town of charm and good cafés and pubs.

Abbreviations and instructions

Instructions are given as concisely as possible to make them easy to follow while you are cycling. Remember to read one or two instructions ahead so that you do not miss a turning. This is most likely to occur when you have to turn off a road on which you have been riding for a fairly long distance and these junctions are marked **Easy to miss** to warn you.

If there appears to be a contradiction between the instructions and what you actually see, always refer to the map. There are many reasons why over the course of a few years instructions will need updating as new roads are built and priorities and signposts change.

If giving instructions for road routes is at times difficult, doing so for off-road routes can often be almost impossible, particularly when the route passes through woodland. With few signposts and buildings by which to orientate yourself, more attention is paid to other features, such as gradient and surface. Most of these routes have been explored between late spring and early autumn and the countryside changes its appearance very dramatically in winter. If in doubt, consult your map and check your compass to see that you are heading in the right direction.

Where I have encountered mud I have mentioned it, but this may change not only from summer to winter but also from dry to wet weather at any time during the year. At times you may have to retrace your steps and find a road alternative.

Some routes have small sections that follow footpaths. The instructions will highlight these sections where you must get off and push your bike. You may only ride on bridleways and by-ways so be careful if you stray from the given routes.

Directions

L	left
LH	left-hand
RH	right-hand
SA	straight ahead or straight across
bear L or R	make less than a 90-degree (right-angle) turn at a fork in the road or track or at a sharp bend so that your course appears to be straight ahead; this is often written as *in effect SA*
sharp L or R turn	is more acute than 90 degrees
sharp R/L back on yourself	an almost U-turn
sharp LH/RH bend	a 90-degree bend
R then L or R	the second turning is visible then immediately L from the first
R then Ist L	the second turning may be some distance from the first; the distance may also be indicated: *R, then after I mile L*

Junctions

T-j	T-junction, a junction where you have to give way
X-roads	crossroads, a junction where you may or may not have to give way
offset X-roads	the four roads are not in the form of a perfect cross and you will have to turn left then right, or vice versa, to continue the route

Signs

'Placename 2'	words in quotation marks are those that appear on signposts; the numbers indicate distance in miles unless stated otherwise
NS	not signposted
trig point	a trigonometrical station

Instructions

An example of an easy instruction is:

4 At the T-j at the end of Smith Road by the White Swan PH R on Brown Street 'Greentown 2, Redville 3'.

There is more information in this instruction than you would normally need, but things do change: pubs may close down and signs may be replaced, removed or vandalized.

An example of a difficult instruction is:

8 Shortly after the brow of the hill, soon after passing a telephone box on the right next L (NS).

As you can see, there is no T-junction to halt you in your tracks, no signpost indicating where the left turn will take you, so you need to have your wits about you in order not to miss the turning.

Fact boxes

The introduction to each route includes a fact box giving useful information:

Start

This is the suggested start point coinciding with instruction I on the map. There is no reason why you should not start at another point if you prefer.

Distance and grade

The distance is, of course, that from the beginning to the end of the route. If you wish to shorten the ride, however, the maps enable you to do so.

The number of drinks bottles indicates the grade:

Easy

Moderate

Strenuous

Page diagrams

The on-road routes occupy four pages of mapping each. The page diagrams on the introductory pages show how the map pages have been laid out, how they overlap and if any inset maps have been used.

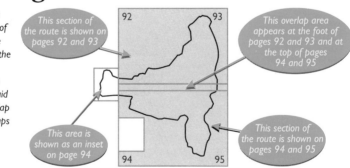

This section of the route is shown on pages 92 and 93

This overlap area appears at the foot of pages 92 and 93 and at the top of pages 94 and 95

This area is shown as an inset on page 94

This section of the route is shown on pages 94 and 95

The grade is based on the amount of climbing involved and, for off-road rides, the roughness of the surface rather than the distance covered.

Remember that conditions may vary dramatically with the weather and seasons, especially along off-road routes

Terrain

This brief description of the terrain may be read in conjunction with the cross-profile diagram at the foot of the page to help you to plan your journey.

Nearest railway

This is the distance to the nearest station from the closest point on the route, not necessarily from the start. Before starting out you should check with British Rail for local restrictions regarding the carrying of bicycles.
(See page 15)

Refreshments

Pubs and teashops on or near the route are listed. The tankard symbols indicate pubs particularly liked by the author

Before you go

Preparing yourself

Fitness

Cycling uses muscles in a different way from walking or running, so if you are beginning or returning to it after a long absence you will need time to train your muscles and become accustomed to sitting on a saddle for a few hours. Build up your fitness and stamina gradually and make sure you are using a bicycle that is the right size for you and suits your needs.

Equipment

Attach the following items to the bike: bell, pump, light-brackets and lights, lock-holder and lock, rack and panniers or elastic straps for securing things to the rack, map holder. Unless it is the middle of summer and the weather is guaranteed to be fine, you will need to carry extra clothes, particularly a waterproof, with you, and it is well worth investing in a rack for this purpose.

Wearing a small pouch around your waist is the easiest and safest way of carrying small tools and personal equipment. The basics are: Allen keys to fit the various Allen bolts on your bike, chainlink extractor, puncture repair kit, reversible screwdriver (slot and crosshead), small adjustable spanner, spare inner tube, tyre levers (not always necessary with mountain bike tyres), coins and a phonecard for food and telephone calls, compass.

Additional tools for extended touring: bottom bracket extractor, cone spanners, freewheel extractor, headset spanners, lubricant, socket spanner for pedals, spare cables, spoke-key.

Clothing

What you wear when you are cycling should be comfortable, allowing you, and most especially your legs, to move freely. It should also be practical, so that it will keep you warm and dry if and when the weather changes.

Feet You can cycle in just about any sort of footwear, but bear in mind that the chain has oil on it, so do not use your very best shoes. Leather tennis shoes or something similar, with a smooth sole to slip into the pedal and toe clip are probably adequate until you buy specialist cycling shoes, which have stiffer soles and are sometimes designed for use with specialist pedals.

Legs Cycling shorts or padded cycling underwear worn under everyday clothing make long rides much more comfortable. Avoid tight, non-stretch trousers, which are very uncomfortable for cycling and will sap your energy, as they restrict the movement of your legs; baggy tracksuit bottoms, which can get caught in the chain and will sag around your ankles if they get wet. Almost anything else will do, though a pair of stretch leggings is probably best.

Upper body What you wear should be long enough to cover your lower back when you are leaning forward and, ideally, should have zips or buttons that you can adjust to regulate your temperature. Several thin layers are better than one thick layer.

Head A helmet may protect your head in a fall.

Wet weather If you get soaked to your skin and you are tired, your body core temperature can drop very quickly when you are cycling. A waterproof, windproof top is essential if it looks like rain. A dustbin bag would be better than nothing but obviously a breathable waterproof material is best.

Cold weather Your extremities suffer far more when you are cycling than when you are walking in similar conditions. A hat that covers your ears, a scarf around your neck, a pair of warm gloves and a thermal top and bottom combined with what you would normally wear cycling should cover almost all conditions.

Night and poor light Wearing light-coloured clothes or reflective strips is almost as important as having lights on your bike. Reflective bands worn around the ankles are particularly effective in making you visible to motorists.

Preparing your bicycle

You may not be a bicycle maintenance expert, but you should make sure that your bike is roadworthy before you begin a ride.

If you are planning to ride in soft, off-road conditions, fit fat, knobbly tyres. If you are using the bike around town or on a road route, fit narrower, smoother tyres.

Check the tyres for punctures or damage and repair or replace if necessary or if you are in any doubt. Keep tyres inflated hard (recommended pressures are on the side wall of the tyre) for mainly on-road riding. You do not need to inflate tyres as hard for off-road use; slightly softer tyres give some cushioning and get better traction in muddy conditions.

Ensure that the brakes work efficiently. Replace worn cables and brake blocks.

The bike should glide along silently. Tighten and adjust any part that is loose or rubbing against a moving part. Using a good-quality bike oil lubricate the hubs, bottom bracket, pedals where they join the cranks, chain and gear-changing mechanism from both sides. If the bike still makes grating noises, replace the bearings.

Adjust the saddle properly. You can raise or lower it, move it forwards or backwards or tilt it up or down. The saddle height should ensure that your legs are working efficiently: too low and your knees will ache; too high and your hips will be rocking in order for your feet to reach the pedals.

Some women find the average bike saddle uncomfortable because the female pelvis is a different shape from the male pelvis and needs a broader saddle for support. Some manufacturers make saddles especially for women.

Cross-profiles

The introduction to each route includes a cross-profile diagram. The vertical scale is the same on each diagram but the horizontal scale varies according to the length of the route

On-road route

Off-road route

Corfe Castle

Start / finish

Blashenwell Farm

Kingston

Swyre Head

Kimmeridge

Tips for touring

England and Wales have 120 000 miles of rights of way, but under the Wildlife and Countryside Act of 1968 you are allowed to cycle on only about 10 percent of them, namely on bridleways, by-ways open to all traffic (BOATS) and roads used as public paths (RUPPS). The other 90 percent of rights of way are footpaths, where you may walk and usually push your bike, but not ride it. Local bylaws sometimes prohibit the pushing of bicycles along footpaths and although all the paths in this book have been checked, bylaws do sometimes change.

⚙ You are not allowed to ride where there is no right of way. If you lose the route and find yourself in conflict with a landowner, stay calm and courteous, make a note of exactly where you are and then contact the Rights of Way Department of the local authority. It has copies of definitive maps and will take up the matter on your behalf if you are in the right.

⚙ For further information on cycling and the law contact the Cyclists Touring Club (CTC) whose address can be found on the inside back cover.

Cycling techniques

If you are not used to cycling more than a few miles at a stretch, you may find initially that touring is tiring. There are ways of conserving your energy, however:

⚙ Do not struggle in a difficult gear if you have an easier one. Let the gears help you up the hills. No matter how many gears a bike has, however, ultimately it is leg power that you need to get you up a hill. You may decide to get off and walk uphill with your bike to rest your muscles.

⚙ You can save a lot of energy on the road by following close behind a stronger rider in his or her slipstream, but do not try this offroad. All the routes are circular, so you can start at any point and follow the instructions until you return to it. This is useful when there is a strong wind, as you can alter the route to go into the wind at the start of the ride, when you are fresh, and have the wind behind you on the return, when you are more tired.

⚙ The main difference in technique between on-road and off-road cycling lies in getting your weight balanced correctly. When going down steep off-road sections, lower the saddle, keep the pedals level, stand up out of the saddle to let your legs absorb the bumps and keep your weight over the rear wheel. Control is paramount: keep your eyes on what lies ahead.

Steeple Hill

Grange Arch

Ridgeway Hill

Knowle Hill

Start / finish

Traffic

The rides in this book are designed to minimize time spent on busy roads, but you will inevitably encounter some traffic. The most effective way to avoid an accident with a motor vehicle is to be highly aware of what is going on around you and to ensure that other road users are aware of you.

- Ride confidently.
- Indicate clearly to other road users what you intend to do, particularly when turning right. Look behind you, wait for a gap in the traffic, indicate, then turn. If you have to turn right off a busy road or on a difficult bend, pull in and wait for a gap in the traffic or go past the turning to a point where you have a clear view of the traffic in both directions, then cross and return to the turning.
- Use your lights and wear reflective clothing at night and in poor light.
- Do not ride two-abreast if there is a vehicle behind you. Let it pass. If it cannot easily overtake you because the road is narrow, look for a passing place or a gate entrance and pull in to let it pass.

Maintenance

Mountain bikes are generally stronger than road bikes, but any bike can suffer. To prevent damage as far as possible:

- Watch out for holes and obstacles.
- Clean off mud and lubricate moving parts regularly.
- Replace worn parts, particularly brake blocks.

Riders also need maintenance:

- Eat before you get hungry, drink before you get thirsty. Dried fruit, nuts and chocolate take up little space and provide lots of energy.

- Carry a water bottle and keep it filled, especially on hot days. Tea, water and well-diluted soft drinks are the best thirst-quenchers.

Breakdowns

The most likely breakdown to occur is a puncture.

- Always carry a pump.
- Take a spare inner tube so that you can leave the puncture repair until later.
- Make sure you know how to remove a wheel. This may require an adjustable spanner or, in many cases, no tool at all, as many bikes now have wheels with quick-release skewers that can be loosened by hand.

Security

Where you park your bike, what you lock it with and what you lock it to are important in protecting it from being stolen.

- Buy the best lock you can afford.
- Lock your bike to something immovable in a well-lit public place.
- Locking two bikes together is better than locking them individually.
- Use a chain with a lock to secure the wheels and saddle to the frame. Keep a note of the frame number and other details, and insure, photograph and code the bike.

Lost and Found

The detailed instructions and the Ordnance Survey mapping in this book minimize the chances of getting lost. However, if you do lose your way:

- Ask someone for directions.
- Retrace the route back to the last point where you knew where you were.
- Use the map to rejoin the route at a point further ahead.

Transporting your bike

There are three ways of getting you and your bike to the start of a ride:

Cycle to the start or to a point along a route near your home.

Take the train. Always check in advance that you can take the bike on the train. Some trains allow only up to two bikes and you may need to make a reservation and pay a flat fee however long the journey. Always label your bike showing your name and destination station.

Travel by motor vehicle. You can carry the bikes:

- Inside the vehicle. With the advent of quick release mechanisms on both wheels and the seatpost, which allow a quick dismantling of the bike, it is possible to fit a bike in even quite small cars. It is unwise to stack one bike on top of another unless you have a thick blanket separating them to prevent scratching or worse damage. If you are standing them up in a van, make sure they are secured so they cannot slide around.

- On top of the vehicle. The advantages of this method are that the bikes are completely out of the way and are not resting against each other, you can get at the boot or hatch easily and the bikes do not obscure the number plate or rear lights and indicators. The disadvantages are that you use up more fuel, the car can feel uncomfortable in a crosswind and you have to be reasonably tall and strong to get the bikes on and off the roof.

- On a rack that attaches to the rear of the vehicle. The advantages are that the rack is easily and quickly assembled and disassembled, fuel consumption is better and anyone can lift the bikes on and off. The disadvantages are that you will need to invest in a separate board carrying the number plate and rear lights if they are obstructed by the bikes, you cannot easily get to the boot or hatch once the bikes have been loaded and secured, and the bikes are resting against each other so you must take care that they don't scrape off paint or damage delicate parts.

- Whichever way you carry the bikes on the outside of the vehicle, ensure that you regularly check that they are secure and that straps and fixings that hold them in place have not come loose. If you are leaving the bikes for any length of time, be sure they are secure against theft; if nothing else lock them to each other.

Code of Conduct

- Enjoy the countryside and respect its life and work
- Only ride where you know you have a legal right
- Always yield to horses and pedestrians
- Take all litter with you
- Don't get annoyed with anyone; it never solves any problems
- Guard against all risk of fire
- Fasten all gates
- Keep your dogs under close control
- Keep to public paths across farmland
- Use gates and stiles to cross fences, hedges and walls
- Avoid livestock, crops and machinery or, if not possible, keep contact to a minimum
- Help keep all water clean
- Protect wildlife, plants and trees
- Take special care on country roads
- Make no unnecessary noise

Legend to 1:50 000 maps

Roads and paths

Motorway

Service area | M 5 | Elevated
Junction number 20

Motorway under construction

Trunk road
Unfenced | Footbridge
A 46 (T)

Main road
Dual carriageway
A 420

Main road under construction

Secondary road
B 4348

Narrow road with passing places
A 855 | B 885

Road generally more than 4 m wide
Bridge

Road generally less than 4 m wide

Other road, drive or track

Path

Gradient: 1 in 5 and steeper, 1 in 7 to 1 in 5

Gates | Road tunnel

Passenger ferry | Vehicle ferry
Ferry P | Ferry V

Public rights of way (Not applicable to Scotland)

· · · · · · · · · · · · Footpath
– – – – – – – Bridleway
–·–·–·–·–·– Road used as a public footpath
–+–+–+–+–+– Byway open to all traffic

Danger Area   Firing and test ranges in the area.
Danger! Observe warning notices

Tourist information

🄸 🄸   Information centre, all year / seasonal
P   Parking
✕   Picnic site
☀   Viewpoint
⋏   Camp site
⌸   Caravan site
▲   Youth hostel
▬   Selected places of tourist interest
✆   Public telephone
✆   Motoring organisation telephone
⚑   Golf course or link
PC   Public convenience (in rural areas)

Railways

Track: multiple or single
Track: narrow gauge
Bridges, footpath
Tunnel
Viaduct
Freight line, siding or tramway
a   b
Station, (a) principal, (b) closed to passengers
Level crossing LC
Embankment
Cutting

Rock features

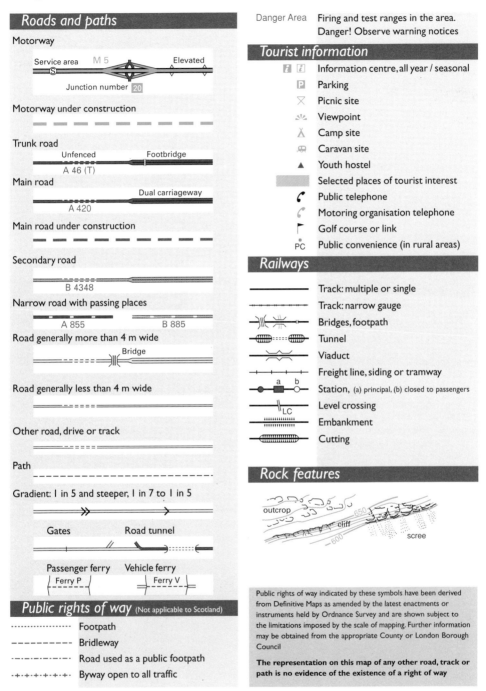

outcrop   cliff   650   600   scree

Public rights of way indicated by these symbols have been derived from Definitive Maps as amended by the latest enactments or instruments held by Ordnance Survey and are shown subject to the limitations imposed by the scale of mapping. Further information may be obtained from the appropriate County or London Borough Council

The representation on this map of any other road, track or path is no evidence of the existence of a right of way

Water features

Canal (dry)

Canal

Lake

Weir Footbridge Bridge

Marsh or salting

Towpath Lock

Aqueduct

Normal tidal limit

Ford

Slopes Cliff High water mark

Flat rock Low water mark

Sand Lighthouse (in use)

Dunes Beacon

Lighthouse (disused)

Mud Shingle

General features

Electricity transmission line
(with pylons spaced conventionally)

Pipeline (arrow indicates direction
of flow)

Buildings

Public buildings (selected)

Bus or coach station

Coniferous wood

Non-coniferous wood

Mixed wood

Orchard

Park or ornamental grounds

Quarry

Spoil heap, refuse tip or dump

Radio or TV mast

Church or chapel with tower

Church or chapel with spire

Church or chapel without
tower or spire

Chimney or tower

Glasshouse

Graticule intersection at 5' intervals

Heliport

Triangulation pillar

Windmill with or without sails

Windpump

Boundaries

National

London borough

National park or forest park

NT open access
National Trust
NT limited access

County, region or islands area

District

Abbreviations

P Post office

PH Public house

MS Milestone

MP Milepost

CH Clubhouse

PC Public convenience (in rural areas)

TH Town hall, guildhall or equivalent

CG Coastguard

Antiquities

VILLA Roman

Castle Non-Roman

Battlefield (with date)

Tumulus

Position of antiquity which cannot be
drawn to scale

Ancient monuments and historic
buildings in the care of the Secretaries
of State for the Environment, for
Scotland and for Wales and that are
open to the public

Heights

50 Contours are at 10 metres vertical
interval

·144 Heights are to the nearest metre
above mean sea level

Heights shown close to a triangulation pillar refer to the station height
at ground level and not necessarily to the summit

17

Leominster to the timber-built villages of Dilwyn, Pembridge and Wigmore

On this ride you will visit the lovely villages of Dilwyn, Pembridge and Wigmore, with their fine black-and-white timbered houses so typical of the Marches country. Quiet sunken lanes through the wooded hillsides between Lingen and Portway provide something of a contrast before the final run back into Leominster.

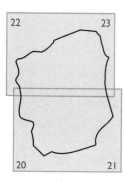

22   23
20   21

Start

Tourist Information Centre, Leominster.

P Follow signs for long-stay car parks

Distance and grade

32 miles

Moderate

Terrain

South of the B4362 the landscape is flat or undulating. North of it there are several hills, the most notable being between Lingen and Wigmore, then between Wigmore and Portway

Nearest railway

Leominster

Refreshments

Royal Oak PH, Talbot PH, plenty of choice in **Leominster**
Crown Inn, **Dilwyn**
New Inn, **Pembridge**
Royal George PH, **Lingen**
Old Oak Inn, **Wigmore**

Leominster   Dorstone   Dilwyn   Luntley   Pembridge   Byton Hand

Leominster 1

In Leominster the streets are laid out in the traditional medieval grid pattern and there are many examples of medieval and Tudor timber-framed buildings. The Priory Church is all that remains of the Benedictine foundation, dissolved in 1539. In the medieval period the town grew and prospered as a wealthy centre trading the wool of the Ryeland sheep known as the 'Lempster Ore'. For 500 years it was one of the great high quality wool markets of England.

▲ *Near Dilwyn*

Dunkertons Cider Company, Luntley 6/7

Traditional cider and perry on sale, made from local cider apples and perry pears.

Old Chapel Gallery, Pembridge 7

Located in East Street the gallery is in a converted Victorian chapel in the heart of this 14th-century village. It has a fine display of art, crafts, designer-made textiles and country furniture.

Croft Castle 20

Originally a Marcher fortress, the ancient walls and four round corner towers date back to the 14th or 15th century and the Georgian Gothic staircase and ceilings were added in the 18th century. The park contains fine specimen trees including oak and beech and an exceptional 350-year-old avenue of Spanish Chestnuts.

Croft Ambrey 20

This is a large Iron Age hill fort above Croft Castle. It lies on the crest of the limestone escarpment from where there are fine views west to the mountains of Wales; on a clear day fourteen counties can be seen.

Lingen

Wigmore

Portway

Luston

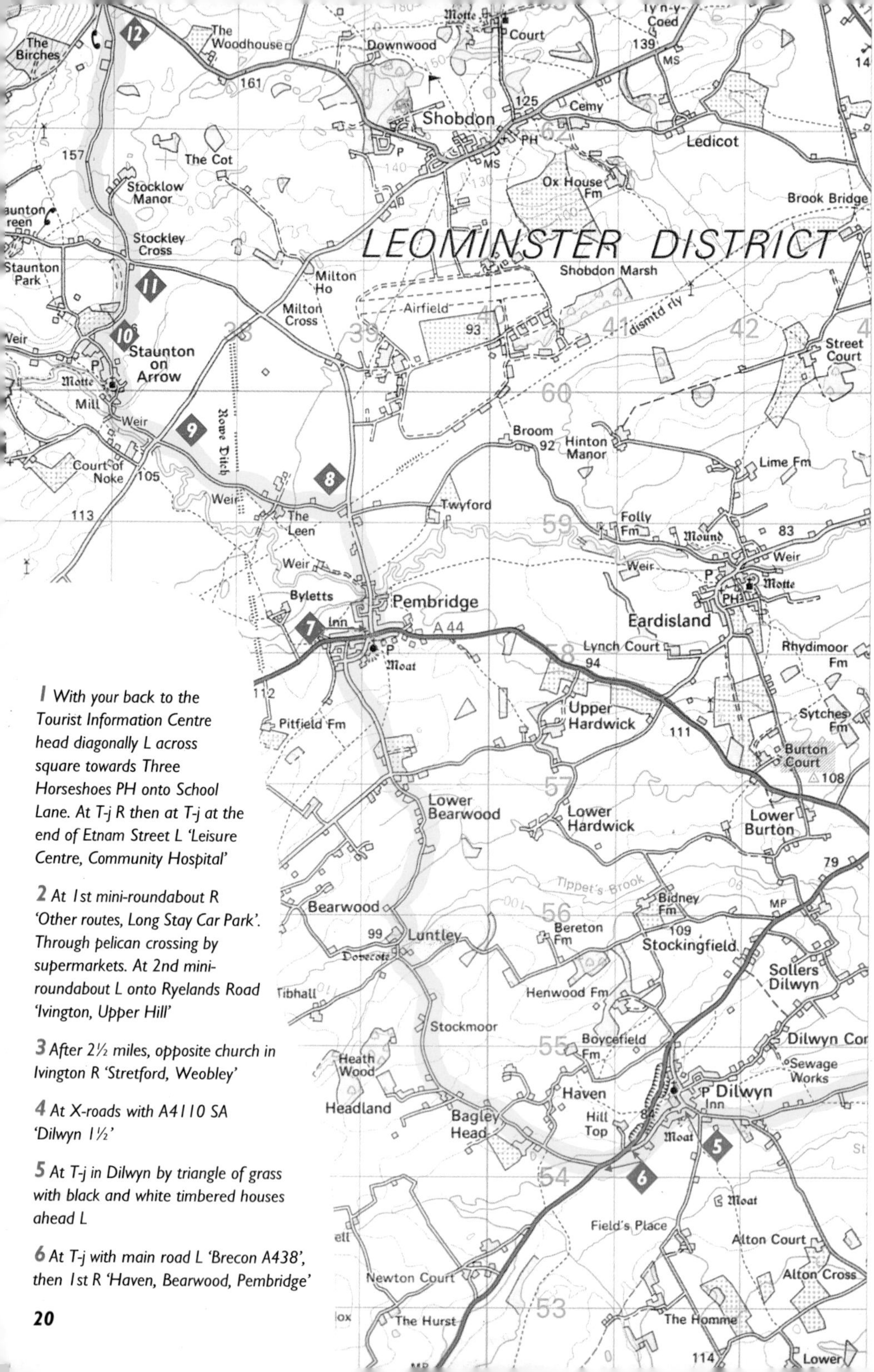

1 With your back to the
Tourist Information Centre
head diagonally L across
square towards Three
Horseshoes PH onto School
Lane. At T-j R then at T-j at the
end of Etnam Street L 'Leisure
Centre, Community Hospital'

2 At 1st mini-roundabout R
'Other routes, Long Stay Car Park'.
Through pelican crossing by
supermarkets. At 2nd mini-
roundabout L onto Ryelands Road
'Ivington, Upper Hill'

3 After 2½ miles, opposite church in
Ivington R 'Stretford, Weobley'

4 At X-roads with A4110 SA
'Dilwyn 1½'

5 At T-j in Dilwyn by triangle of grass
with black and white timbered houses
ahead L

6 At T-j with main road L 'Brecon A438',
then 1st R 'Haven, Bearwood, Pembridge'

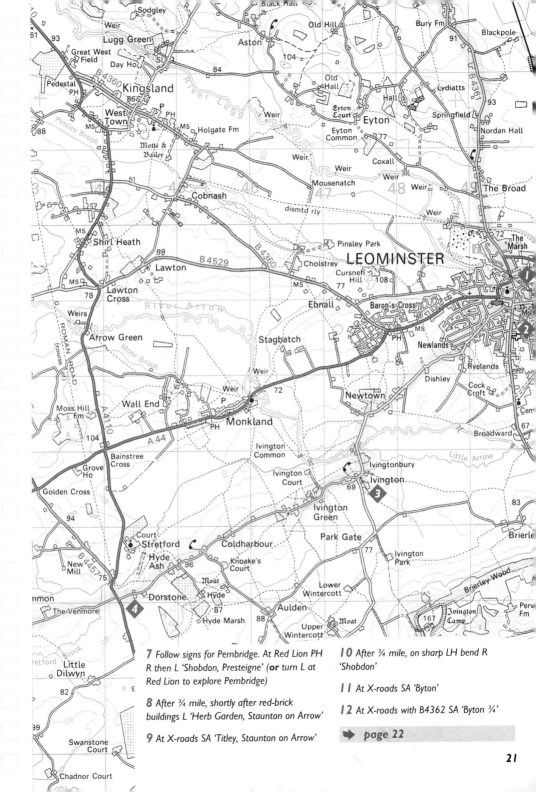

7 Follow signs for Pembridge. At Red Lion PH R then L 'Shobdon, Presteigne' (**or** turn L at Red Lion to explore Pembridge)

8 After ¾ mile, shortly after red-brick buildings L 'Herb Garden, Staunton on Arrow'

9 At X-roads SA 'Titley, Staunton on Arrow'

10 After ¾ mile, on sharp LH bend R 'Shobdon'

11 At X-roads SA 'Byton'

12 At X-roads with B4362 SA 'Byton ¾'

➡ page 22

12 At X-roads with B4362 SA 'Byton ¾'

13 Up and over hill through woodland. Cross bridge, climb hill and 1st R uphill by steep triangle of grass

14 In Lingen, shortly after Royal George PH, on sharp LH bend R 'Dickendale, Wigmore'

15 After 4 miles at T-j with A4110 at the bottom of hill L 'Knighton', then 1st R through Wigmore by Ye Old Oak Inn 'Ludlow'

16 Easy to miss. After 3 miles, on sharp LH bend R 'Richards Castle'

17 Easy to miss. After 2½ miles, at the bottom of a hill by a triangle of grass R 'Portway, Woofferton'

18 At T-j R (NS). (Orleton and Woofferton are signposted to the left)

19 At X-roads by Maidenhead PH R.

20 On sharp LH bend after 1¼ miles L 'Leominster, Luston B4361' to return to Leominster

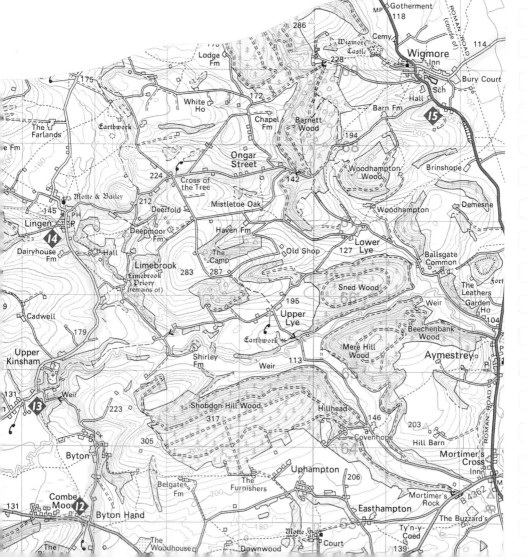

2 East from Leominster to Bromyard

Explore the rolling hills of Hereford and Worcestershire between Leominster and Bromyard on this ride. Taking you along quiet lanes, with the minimum time spent on major roads, it celebrates the fact that much of the countryside in this part of England remains relatively untouched by the late 20th century. This ride can easily be linked with routes one, three and four.

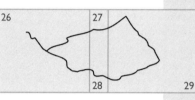

Start

Tourist Information Centre, Leominster

P Follow signs for long-stay car parks.

Distance and grade

27 miles

Moderate

Terrain

Two steep climbs of 200 and 330 feet either side of Risbury and a more gentle one of 330 feet north from Bromyard to the cryptic Hampton Charles

Nearest railway

Leominster

Refreshments

Royal Oak PH, Talbot PH, plenty of choice in **Leominster**
Lamb Inn, **Stoke Prior**
Crown and Sceptre PH, plenty of choice in **Bromyard**

Leominster   Stoke Prior   Risbury   Pencombe   Bromyard   Instone

Shortwood Dairy Farm, Pencombe 8
Ideal for children. Feed the calves and pigs, watch the milking and see wool being sheared, spun and woven.

Lower Brockhampton Manor 10
This house is situated away from the route at instruction 10, off the A44. It is a fine 15th-century timber-framed house of rare interest because it is protected by its own moat. Access is by a small bridge under the timbered gate-house.

▲ Leominster

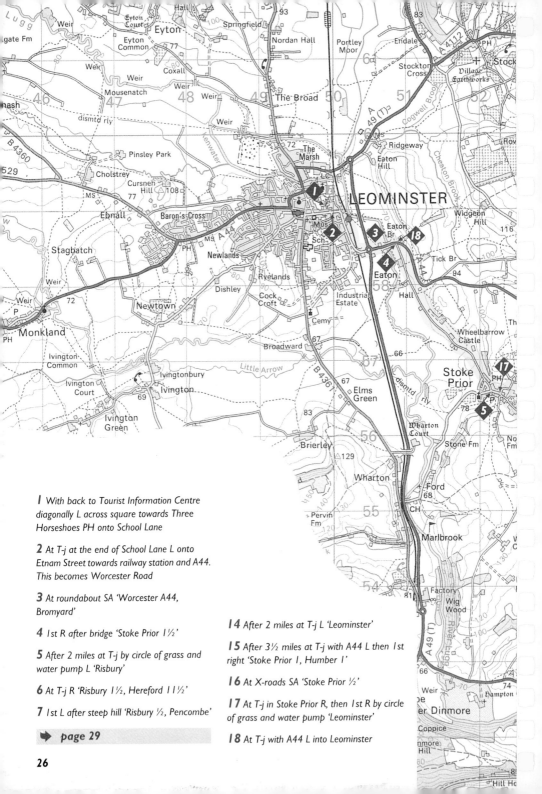

1 With back to Tourist Information Centre diagonally L across square towards Three Horseshoes PH onto School Lane

2 At T-j at the end of School Lane L onto Etnam Street towards railway station and A44. This becomes Worcester Road

3 At roundabout SA 'Worcester A44, Bromyard'

4 1st R after bridge 'Stoke Prior 1½'

5 After 2 miles at T-j by circle of grass and water pump L 'Risbury'

6 At T-j R 'Risbury 1½, Hereford 11½'

7 1st L after steep hill 'Risbury ½, Pencombe'

➡ **page 29**

14 After 2 miles at T-j L 'Leominster'

15 After 3½ miles at T-j with A44 L then 1st right 'Stoke Prior 1, Humber 1'

16 At X-roads SA 'Stoke Prior ½'

17 At T-j in Stoke Prior R, then 1st R by circle of grass and water pump 'Leominster'

18 At T-j with A44 L into Leominster

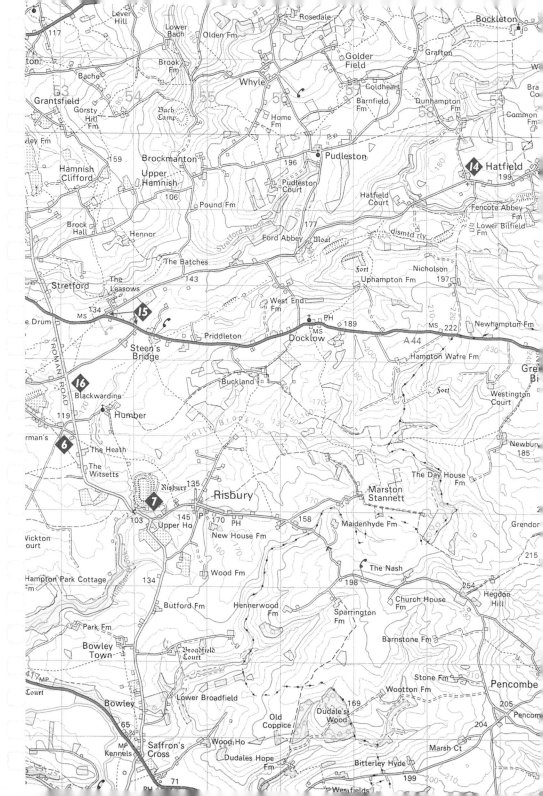

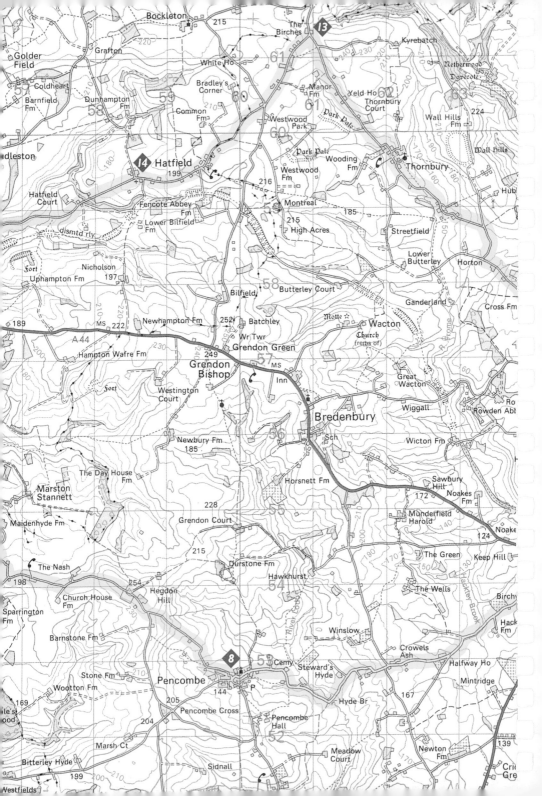

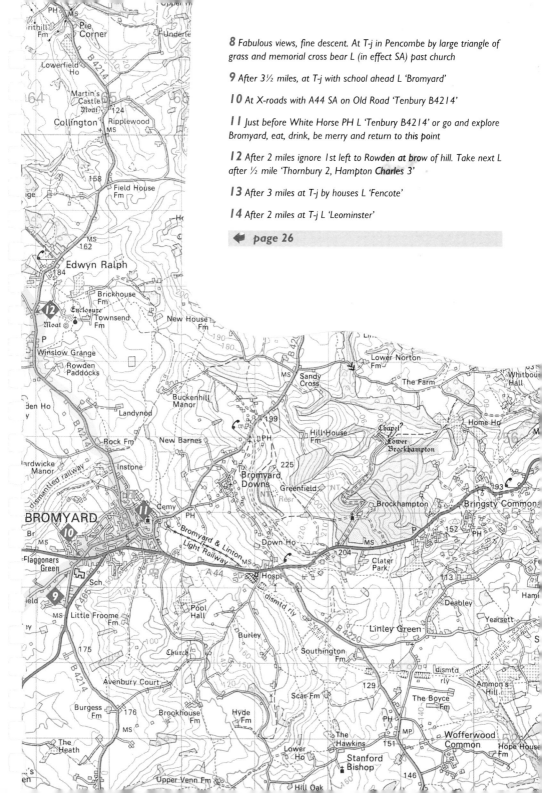

8 *Fabulous views, fine descent. At T-j in Pencombe by large triangle of grass and memorial cross bear L (in effect SA) past church*

9 *After 3½ miles, at T-j with school ahead L 'Bromyard'*

10 *At X-roads with A44 SA on Old Road 'Tenbury B4214'*

11 *Just before White Horse PH L 'Tenbury B4214' or go and explore Bromyard, eat, drink, be merry and return to this point*

12 *After 2 miles ignore 1st left to Rowden at brow of hill. Take next L after ½ mile 'Thornbury 2, Hampton Charles 3'*

13 *After 3 miles at T-j by houses L 'Fencote'*

14 *After 2 miles at T-j L 'Leominster'*

← **page 26**

3 From Tenbury Wells to Clifton upon Teme, returning via the Teme Valley

*F*or a ride through a very beautiful, unspoilt part of the north of Hereford and Worcester, you start in Tenbury Wells, a small, attractive town typical of the area. A long climb south from Little Hereford brings you to Leysters Pole, the first of several high points along the outward part of the route. You will enjoy the best views of the ride from the top of the next hill – Kyre Green. The valley you see before you from this pinnacle is the one from which you will have to climb very steeply at Upper Underley. Just when you thought you deserved an easy run into Clifton, you are faced with another climb. This time your reward is a long, exhilarating descent to the bottom of the river valley, which you follow westwards over many an up and down back to Tenbury Wells.

Start

Tourist Information Centre, Tenbury Wells

P Follow signs

Distance and grade

35 miles

Moderate/strenuous

Terrain

Lots of hills – even the route along the valley is full of ups and downs. A 450-foot climb from the Teme River near Little Hereford to Leysters Pole, 290 feet from Cockspur Hall to Kyre Green, a savage little number at Upper Underley and an ascent of 290 feet to Clifton

Nearest railway

Leominster, 6 miles from Leysters, or Ludlow, 6 miles from Tenbury Wells

Refreshments

Fountain PH ✦, Ship PH ✦, plenty of choice in **Tenbury Wells**
Red Lion PH **Clifton upon Teme**

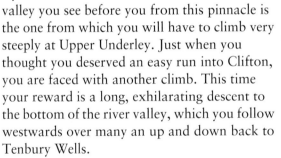

Burford Tenbury Wells Berrington Stony Cross Leysters Pole Cockspur Hall Bockleton Kyre Green Upper Underley Thr...tes

Burford 1

Burford lies in Shropshire and joins Tenbury Wells at Teme Bridge which marks the boundaries of the two counties. The church at Burford has several monuments to the Cornewall family, who held the barony of Burford from 1304 to 1726. One of these is the tomb of Princess Elizabeth, sister of King Henry IV who died in 1426.

Tenbury Wells 2

Market town on the banks of the Teme known as the 'Town in the Orchard' renowned for its hops, fruit, holly and mistletoe. Spa water was discovered in 1839 and the Spa building was built in 1862. The pump room and baths, though long disused, can still be seen.

▲ Tenbury Wells

Burford House Gardens 2/3

1 mile West of Tenbury Wells this is a garden noted for its marvellous collection of plants. The many rare and unusual trees, shrubs and plants have been collected during the last 30 years.

Leysters 6

The Poet's Stone carved with the initials W.W and M.W stands near the Church. The initials are those of William Wordsworth and Mary Hutchinson who lived in a nearby parish and married in 1802.

Clifton upon Teme

Stanford Bridge

Orleton

Rochford

1 With your back to the Tourist Information Centre R out of town on the A4112 'Bromyard, Leominster'

2 100 yards after a sharp LH bend, just past an Indian restaurant R on Berrington Road past the Police Station

3 After 1½ miles, at T-j with red-brick barn ahead R 'Little Hereford'

4 After 2 miles at T-j L 'Middleton on the Hill, Leysters'

5 Easy to miss After 2½ miles, having ignored a left turn to Upton, on a gentle downhill stretch turn L uphill 'Leysters' on a lane parallel with a rough track

6 Steep climb. At X-roads with A4112 SA (NS)

7 At T-j after 2 miles L 'Tenbury'

8 At next T-j R 'Bromyard 7, Hampton Charles 1, Hatfield 2'

9 At top of gentle climb, just past Bockleton church (set back to the right), with a stone cross on your left L 'Kyre, Thornbury'

10 At T-j by triangle of grass L 'Kyre'

11 Savour the views! Steep descent. At T-j R 'Bromyard'

12 After 1 mile, shortly past a telephone box on your right L 'Hanley 4, Stoke Bliss Church'

➡ **page 35**

19 Follow signs for Lower Rochford, then Tenbury for 3½ miles

20 At T-j R 'Tenbury', then R again at T-j with A4112 in Tenbury to return to Tourist Information Centre

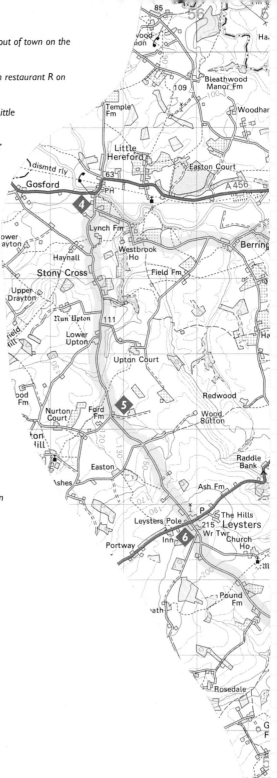

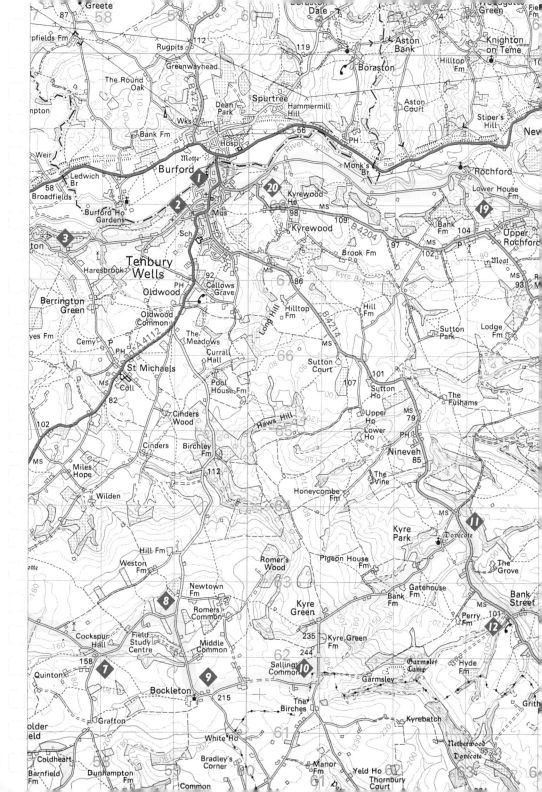

11 *Savour the views! Steep descent. At T-j R 'Bromyard'*

12 *After 1 mile, shortly past a telephone box on your right L 'Hanley 4, Stoke Bliss Church'*

13 *Follow signs for Wolferlow up a brutish hill! (Good excuse for walking – excellent views back to the right as you climb the hill!) At X-roads with B4203 SA (NS)*

14 *At T-j with B4204 in Clifton upon Teme at the end of Hope Lane R 'Martley, Worcester' (or L for stores)*

15 *Steep descent. Just before reaching the bridge over the Teme L 'The Shelsleys, Stanford'*

16 *After 4 miles, at T-j with B4203 L 'Bromyard 9½'*

17 *After ¾ mile, just before church up on the hill to the left, 1st R 'Orleton, Eastham'*

18 Easy to miss. *Follow for 3 miles. ½ mile after telephone box on the right opposite modern red-brick houses, on a sharp RH bend, bear L (in effect SA) 'Highwood'*

19 *Follow signs for Lower Rochford then Tenbury for 3½ miles*

← **page 32**

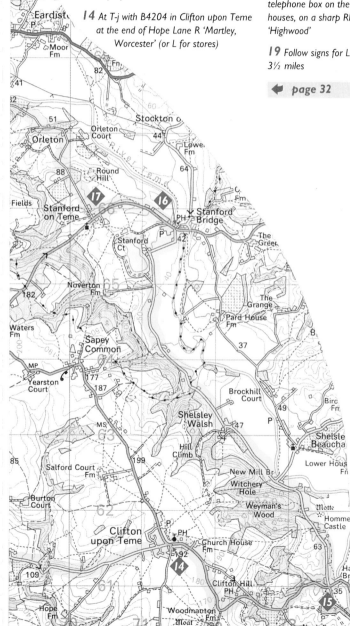

4 *From Ledbury to Bromyard, beneath the Malvern Hills*

Starting from the historic and picturesque town of Ledbury, with its fine black-and-white buildings, this ride offers some fine views of the Malverns without actually climbing them. Bromyard is the obvious stopping point, with plenty to see and a wide choice of grazing opportunities. On the way back the route follows the delightful River Frome southwards before climbing over Fromes Hill and dropping back down to Ledbury.

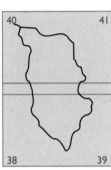

Start

The Market Hall, Ledbury

P Follow signs for long-stay car parks

Distance and grade

30 miles

Easy/moderate

Terrain

Two climbs worth noting, one of 230 feet at the start, between Ledbury and Kilbury Camp, and a second one of 350 feet close to the end at Fromes Hill

Nearest railway

Ledbury

Refreshments

Feathers PH ● ●, Olde Talbot ●, plenty of choice, **Ledbury**
Crown and Sceptre PH ●, plenty of choice, **Bromyard**
Cliffe Arms PH ●, **Mathon**
Green Dragon PH ●, **Bishop's Frome** (just off the route between instructions 15 and 16)
Oak PH ●, **Staplow**

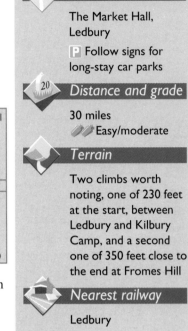

Ledbury Kilbury Camp Colwall Grittlesend Suckley

Ledbury *1*

Ledbury is a small, ancient market town west of the Malvern Hills that is characterised by the numerous half-timbered houses. The Market House, built as a corn market, stands clear of the ground on massive timber pillars and the space beneath is still used for

market stalls. Church Lane in Ledbury is a well-preserved, cobbled street that has been used many times in period dramas. The old grammar school in Church Lane is now the heritage centre where the town's development is traced from Anglo-Saxon village to market town. Two famous writers have connections with Ledbury: John Masefield was brought up in Ledbury and Elizabeth Barret Browning lived a few miles away and was commemorated by the clock tower in the town's centre.

▲ *Ledbury*

Eastnor Castle *2*

This is situated 1½ miles southeast of Ledbury off the route at instruction 2. Medieval in appearance, with dramatic turrets and towers, it is in fact less than 200 years old. Inside there is a fine collection of armour, pictures and tapestries and Italian furniture. There is also an arboretum, lake and deer park.

B4220   Bromyard   Mayfields Farm   Fromes Hill   Catley Southfield

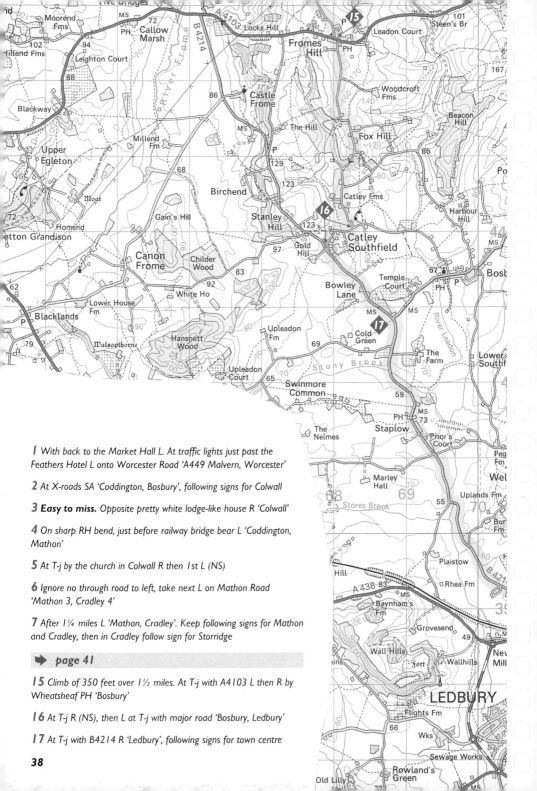

1 With back to the Market Hall L. At traffic lights just past the Feathers Hotel L onto Worcester Road 'A449 Malvern, Worcester'

2 At X-roads SA 'Coddington, Bosbury', following signs for Colwall

3 **Easy to miss.** Opposite pretty white lodge-like house R 'Colwall'

4 On sharp RH bend, just before railway bridge bear L 'Coddington, Mathon'

5 At T-j by the church in Colwall R then 1st L (NS)

6 Ignore no through road to left, take next L on Mathon Road 'Mathon 3, Cradley 4'

7 After 1¼ miles L 'Mathon, Cradley'. Keep following signs for Mathon and Cradley, then in Cradley follow sign for Storridge

➡ *page 41*

15 Climb of 350 feet over 1½ miles. At T-j with A4103 L then R by Wheatsheaf PH 'Bosbury'

16 At T-j R (NS), then L at T-j with major road 'Bosbury, Ledbury'

17 At T-j with B4214 R 'Ledbury', following signs for town centre

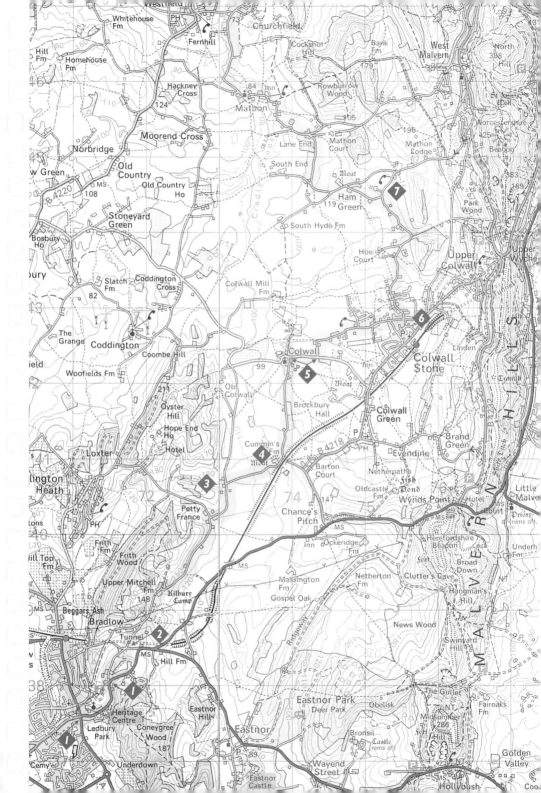

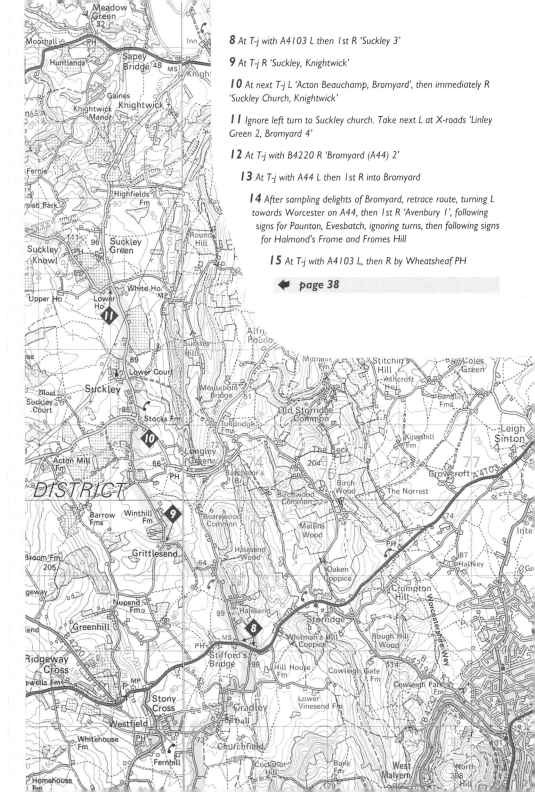

8 At T-j with A4103 L then 1st R 'Suckley 3'

9 At T-j R 'Suckley, Knightwick'

10 At next T-j L 'Acton Beauchamp, Bromyard', then immediately R 'Suckley Church, Knightwick'

11 Ignore left turn to Suckley church. Take next L at X-roads 'Linley Green 2, Bromyard 4'

12 At T-j with B4220 R 'Bromyard (A44) 2'

13 At T-j with A44 L then 1st R into Bromyard

14 After sampling delights of Bromyard, retrace route, turning L towards Worcester on A44, then 1st R 'Avenbury 1', following signs for Paunton, Evesbatch, ignoring turns, then following signs for Halmond's Frome and Fromes Hill

15 At T-j with A4103 L, then R by Wheatsheaf PH

← **page 38**

5 *From Hay-on-Wye to Kington and back via the Wye Valley*

Hay-on-Wye is a real delight for all lovers of good books, good food and lovely countryside. The ride heads north out of Hay and through Clifford to cross the Wye on a toll bridge. There follows a long, steady climb out of the valley via Brilley and Brilley Mountain, where the road runs along the border between England and Wales. At this point there are superb views down into the Wye Valley to the right and over the valley of the River Arrow to Hergest Ridge to the left. Kington is a typical Welsh Borders town, with wooden timbered houses and several pubs and cafés. From here the ride crosses and recrosses the River Arrow before continuing along some lovely

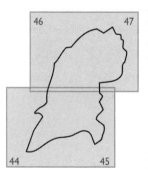

stretches on tiny, quiet lanes in the flat countryside formed by the Wye. Having crossed the Wye near Bredwardine, the route now follows the B4352 over Pen-y-Park hill back to Hay.

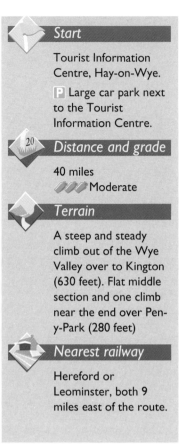

Start

Tourist Information Centre, Hay-on-Wye.

P Large car park next to the Tourist Information Centre.

Distance and grade

40 miles

Moderate

Terrain

A steep and steady climb out of the Wye Valley over to Kington (630 feet). Flat middle section and one climb near the end over Pen-y-Park (280 feet)

Nearest railway

Hereford or Leominster, both 9 miles east of the route.

Hay-on-Wye   Clifford   River Wye   Brilley   Kington   Shawl

Hay-on-Wye 1

Hay-on-Wye stands on the Breconshire side of the River Wye. Its name is of Norman origin, Hay or Haia meaning a fenced or hedged enclosure. The Norman Marcher Lord, William de Breos II built the castle around 1200; much of it was destroyed in the 15th century by folk hero Owain Glyndwr but a fine gateway, the keep and parts of the wall remain. The town is renowned worldwide for its second-hand book trade and there are some 20 major independent bookshops.

Refreshments

Black Lion PH ❤❤*, plenty of choice in* **Hay-on-Wye**
Plenty of choice in **Kington**
Rhydspence PH ❤❤*,* **Whitney-on-Wye** *(just off the route near instruction 3)*

Hay-on-Wye Craft Centre 1

A purpose built craft centre situated on Oxford Road where craftsmen can be seen at work. Crafts include woodturning, ceramics, jewellery, glass, leather, dried flowers and designer clothes.

Clifford Castle 2

The remains of an 11th-century castle comprising gatehouse, hall and round towers situated 2 miles northeast of Hay-on-Wye.

Hergest Croft Gardens 6

Just on the map near instruction 6 this is a garden for all seasons with magnolias, azaleas, lilies, roses, hydrangeas and rhododendrons plus a fine collection of trees and shrubs surrounding an Edwardian house.

Kington 7

'Chingtune', in the Domesday Book of 1086, is said to have derived its name from two Old English words meaning 'royal manor' or 'royal town'. It has many houses that are at least 300 hundred years old. The Crooked Well, once the source of the town's water supply, was famed for its cures of ulcers and sore eyes.

Weston   Woonton   Almeley   Kinnersley   Bredwardine   Pen-y-Park

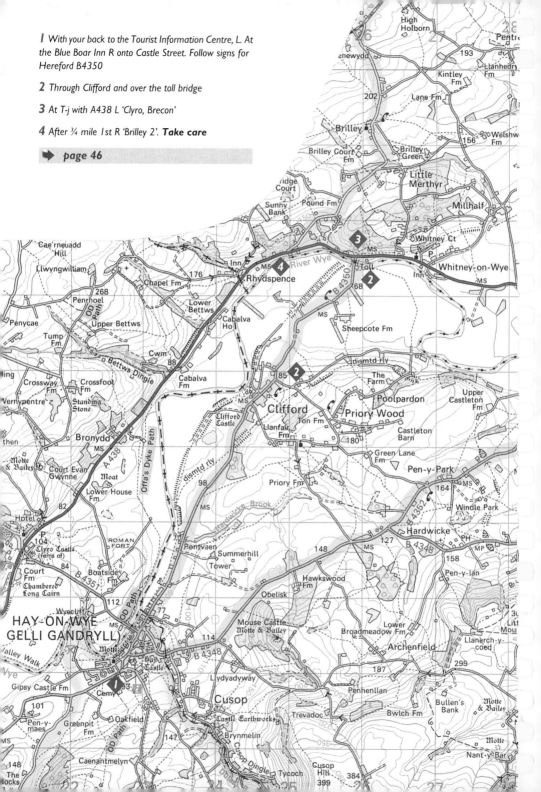

1 With your back to the Tourist Information Centre, L. At the Blue Boar Inn R onto Castle Street. Follow signs for Hereford B4350

2 Through Clifford and over the toll bridge

3 At T-j with A438 L 'Clyro, Brecon'

4 After ¾ mile 1st R 'Brilley 2'. **Take care**

➡ **page 46**

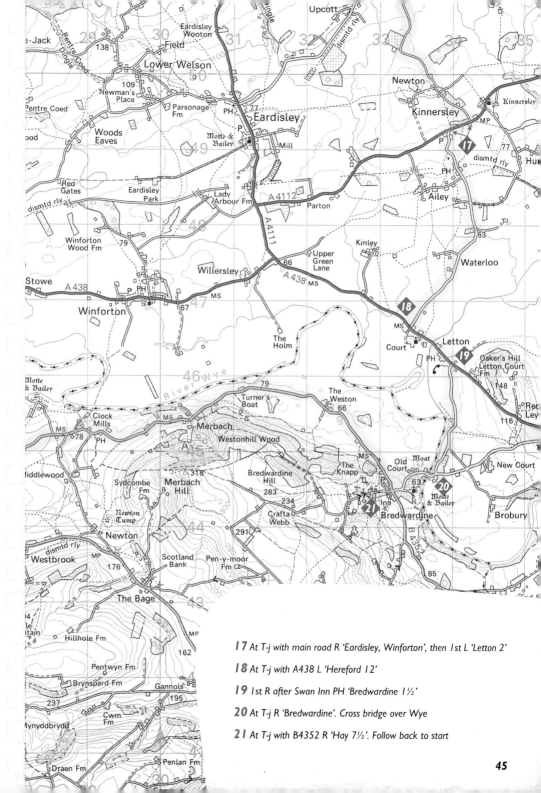

17 At T-j with main road R 'Eardisley, Winforton', then 1st L 'Letton 2'

18 At T-j with A438 L 'Hereford 12'

19 1st R after Swan Inn PH 'Bredwardine 1½'

20 At T-j R 'Bredwardine'. Cross bridge over Wye

21 At T-j with B4352 R 'Hay 7½'. Follow back to start

45

5 Follow signs for Brilley then Kington for 6 miles

6 At T-j R 'Kington Town Centre'

7 Follow road through Kington. At a sharp RH bend by the bank, Post Office and Library, bear L (in effect SA)

8 At roundabout take the B4355 'Presteigne'

9 After 3 miles, shortly after the sign for Titley R downhill 'Whittern, Lyonshall', then soon 1st L (NS)

10 At offset X-roads by telephone box R 'Lyonshall'

11 After 1 mile ignore 1st left by triangle of grass and power lines. Shortly at T-j with more major road L 'Shobdon' then 1st R 'Marston'

12 At T-j with A44 R then 1st L 'Weston, Bearwood, Broxwood'

13 At T-j R 'Broxwood'

14 Follow signs for Hereford over a X-roads, then 1st R beneath a 4-way telegraph pole (NS)

15 At T-j with A480 R then 1st L 'Almeley'

16 Follow signs for Kinnersley, Eardisley past village green and at T-j with shop ahead L 'Kinnersley, Eardisley' and follow signs for Kinnersley

← **page 45**

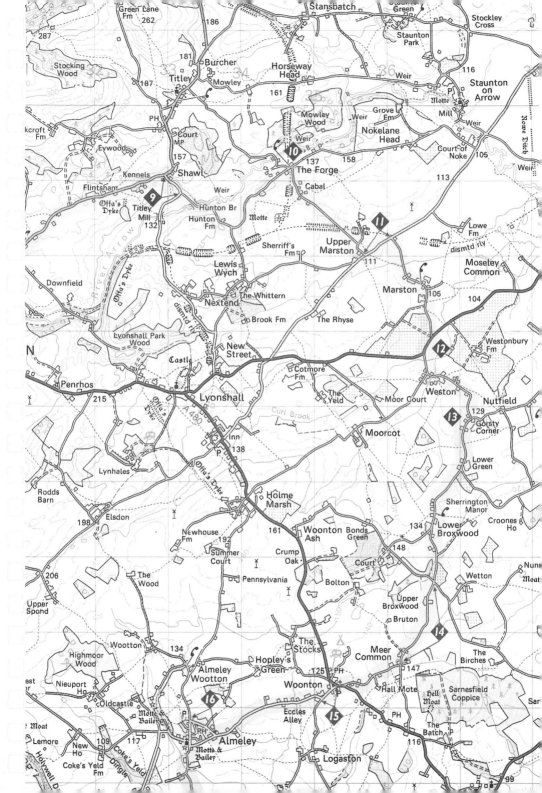

A stiff challenge on the Black Mountains, south of Hay-on-Wye

Every now and then it is good to set yourself a tough cycling challenge and this is certainly one! If you can see through the sweat, there are some magnificent views. The route leaves the easy pleasures of bookshops and cafés in Hay-on-Wye and soon starts to climb up onto the eastern flanks of the Black Mountains. After 3½ miles you have climbed over 1200 feet to the highest point of the ride at 1470 feet. There are fine views across to Hay Bluff to your right. The ride follows the valley of the River Monnow down to Longtown, the start of the second climb, a mere 350 feet up over the hill to Ewyas Harold. The run through the Golden Valley will seem positively tame, so from the delightful village green and the very fine Pandy Inn in Dorstone you can either go for the soft option via the B4348 or, if you are a purist (or masochist), once again climb over the hills via Archenfield (500 feet) to swoop down into Hay.

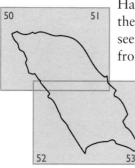

Start

Tourist Information Centre, Hay-on-Wye

P Large car park next to Tourist Information Centre

Distance and grade

32 miles

Strenuous

Terrain

A short stretch along the Golden Valley, sandwiched among an awful lot of hills

Nearest railway

Hereford, 9 miles from the route at Vowchurch or Abergavenny, 9 miles from the route at Longtown

Hay-on-Wye   The Birches   Craswall   Longtown   Ewyas Harc

Ewyas Harold 7

This village was recorded in the Domesday Book as one of only five boroughs in the county. The motte and bailey castle was originally built by one of the Marcher Lords, Osbert Pentecost to defend the border against the marauding Welsh. The common here is a good place to stop for a picnic.

Refreshments

Black Lion PH ❦❦, plenty of choice in **Hay-on-Wye**
Bull's Head Inn, **Craswall**
Crown Inn, **Longtown**
Dog PH, Temple Bar PH, **Ewyas Harold**
Pandy Inn ❦❦, **Dorstone**
Neville Arms PH ❦, **Abbey Dore**

Dore Abbey 7

Just north of Ewyas Harold are the remains of Dore Abbey a 12th-century Cistercian monastery. It was initially occupied by French monks and their community but after the dissolution it deteriorated into near ruins. Restoration eventually took place in the 17th century and since then it has served the surrounding community as a parish church.

Abbey Dore Court Garden 7

Located just off the route and over the river at Abbey Dore, there is a walled garden with shrubs and herbaceous borders, a herb garden and plants for sale. The gardens also have 'The Country Gift Gallery' and 'The Bear's Loft' which has a wide range of bear paraphernalia and limited edition and collector's teddy bears for sale. Morning coffee, light lunches and cream teas are served in 'The Stables'.

Abbey Dore · River Dore · Peterchurch · Dorstone · B4348

1 With your back to the Tourist Information Centre L, then at the Blue Boar Inn L on Castle Street, heading out of town on the B4350 towards Brecon and Builth

2 After 400 yards, on a sharp RH bend, L on Forest Road 'Capel y ffin'

3 650 feet climb. After 2½ miles by a triangle of grass L 'Craswall 4'

➡ **page 52**

9 At X-roads in Peterchurch L 'Urishay, Fairfield School'

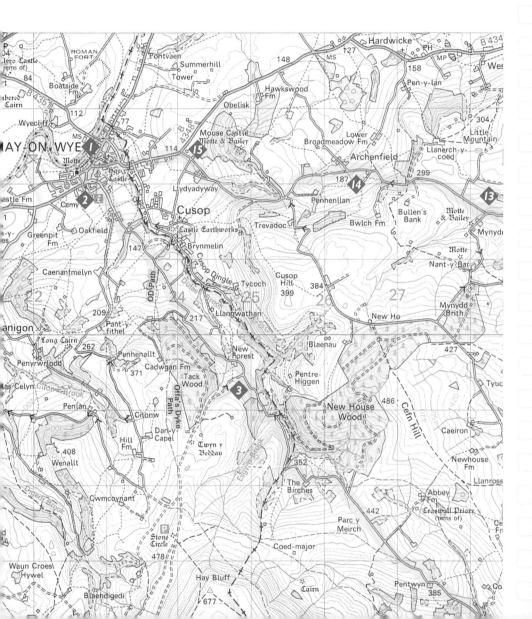

10 1st R 'Fairfield High School'

11 Through Dorstone, following signs for Hay

12 At T-j L 'Mynydd Brith' (easy option: follow B4348 into Hay)

13 460 feet climb over 3 miles, following signs for Archenfield, Cusop

14 After steep descent, on sharp RH bend, L 'Cusop, Hay-on-Wye'.
140 feet climb. At T-j R 'Hay-on-Wye'

15 At T-j with B4348 L into Hay-on-Wye

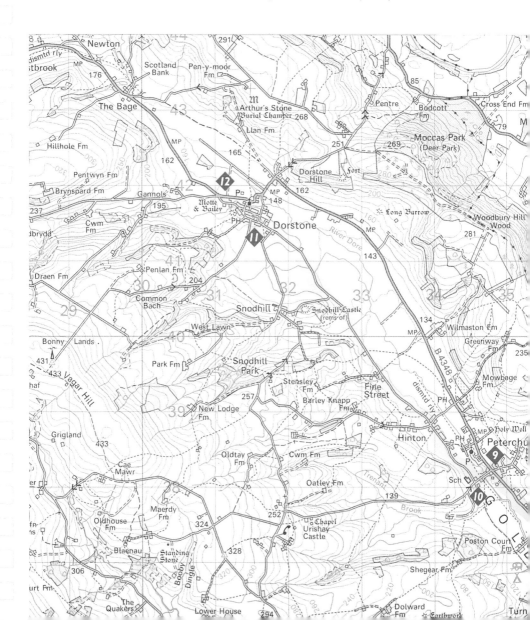

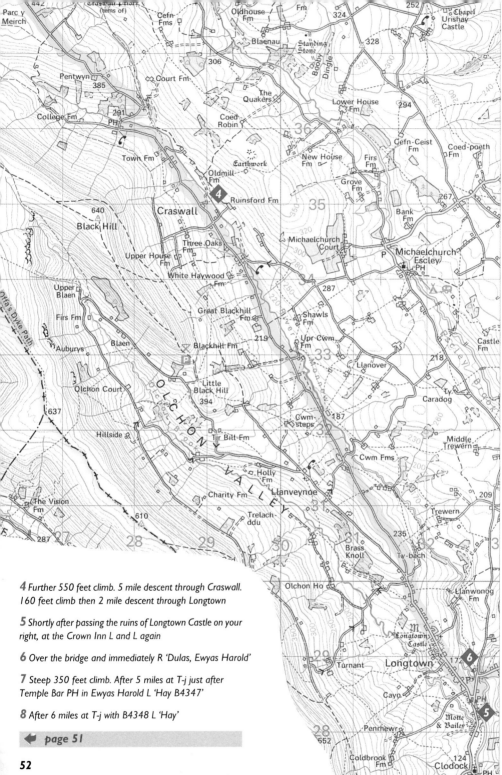

4 Further 550 feet climb. 5 mile descent through Craswall. 160 feet climb then 2 mile descent through Longtown

5 Shortly after passing the ruins of Longtown Castle on your right, at the Crown Inn L and L again

6 Over the bridge and immediately R 'Dulas, Ewyas Harold'

7 Steep 350 feet climb. After 5 miles at T-j just after Temple Bar PH in Ewyas Harold L 'Hay B4347'

8 After 6 miles at T-j with B4348 L 'Hay'

◀ **page 51**

North from Ross-on-Wye, following the loops of the River Wye

This is a delightful ride that does not go anywhere specific but follows the River Wye as closely as possible on minor roads north of Ross. There are some lovely stretches right next to the river near

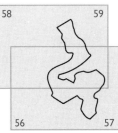

Hoarwithy, How Caple and Hole-in-the-Wall, and any climb opens up big views within this beautiful valley. Add to all this a selection of very fine pubs on both sides of the river and you have a real jewel of a ride.

Start

The Market Hall, Ross-on-Wye

P Long-stay parking on Wilton Road (the road out of town towards Hereford and Monmouth)

Distance and grade

31 miles

Easy/moderate

Terrain

Basically flat, with a few short, sharp climbs, the worst by far being the 270-foot climb up through Capler Wood, south of Fownhope

Nearest railway

Hereford, 5 miles from the route at the bridge over the Wye northeast of Holme Lacy

Refreshments

Hope & Anchor PH ✦✦, plenty of choice, **Ross-on-Wye**
Loughpool PH ✦✦, New Harp Inn ✦, **Hoarwithy**
Cottage of Content PH ✦✦, **Carey**
Green Man PH ✦, Forge and Ferry PH, **Fownhope**

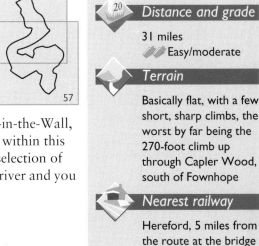

Ross-on-Wye

Bridstow

Baysham

Hoarwithy

Ballingham

Holme Lacy

Fownhope

Ross-on-Wye /

A market town in the heart of the Wye valley. 'Ross' is the Welsh word for 'promontory' or 'headland' which accurately describes the town built on a sandstone cliff overlooking a loop in the river Wye. St Mary's church dating from the 13th century has an impressive 208-foot spire towering above the town while an important feature of the High Street is the red-sandstone market hall, built in 1660, standing in the centre of the town on stone pillars.

▲ Ross-on-Wye

Lost Street Museum, Ross-on-Wye /

Located in Brookend Street the museum is an Edwardian Street with authentic shops containing collections of toys, dolls, musical boxes, gramophones, radios, motorcycles and thousands of advertising items of the period.

Capler Wood

King's Caple

Sellack Boat

How Caple

Brampton Abbotts

1 Take the road along the top end of the market hall past the shop and the King's Head PH on the road towards Monmouth and Hereford

2 At roundabout with A40 SA 'Hereford A49'

3 1st R 'Backney, Foy, Strangford'

4 After 2 miles, having passed the Golf Course on your left and a row of pine trees on your right, at the bottom of a fast hill on a sharp RH bend turn L 'Hoarwithy 4, Hereford 11'

5 At X-roads in Sellack by memorial cross R 'Hoarwithy'

6 Follow signs for Hoarwithy past the Loughpool PH. In Hoarwithy 1st R after New Harp Inn 'King's Caple 1, Carey 1½', then 1st L 'Carey, Ballingham' (*or*, for short ride, do not turn left but go SA, cross the river and take the 1st R rejoining route at instruction 13)

➡ **page 58**

11 At X-roads R 'Hoarwithy' (For shorter route, SA at X-roads 'How Caple, Foy'. Rejoin route at instruction 17, going SA at X-roads)

12 At T-j R (NS) then 1st L by junction of telephone wires 'Ruxton'

13 At X-roads just past church in King's Caple R 'Sellack Boat'

14 At T-j by triangle of grass with drive to Poulstone Court to your right turn R (NS)

15 At T-j by triangle of grass and large red barn R 'How Caple'

16 At T-j with lovely red sandstone house ahead R 'How Caple, Ross-on-Wye, Ledbury'

17 **Easy to miss.** After 2 miles, at X-roads (your priority) R 'Ross-on-Wye'

18 Follow this road for 5 miles, over the dual carriageway, back into Ross

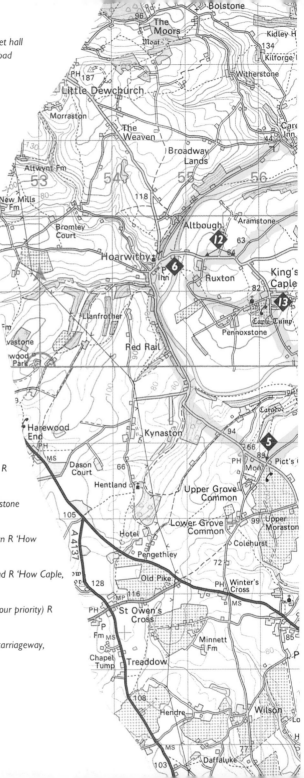

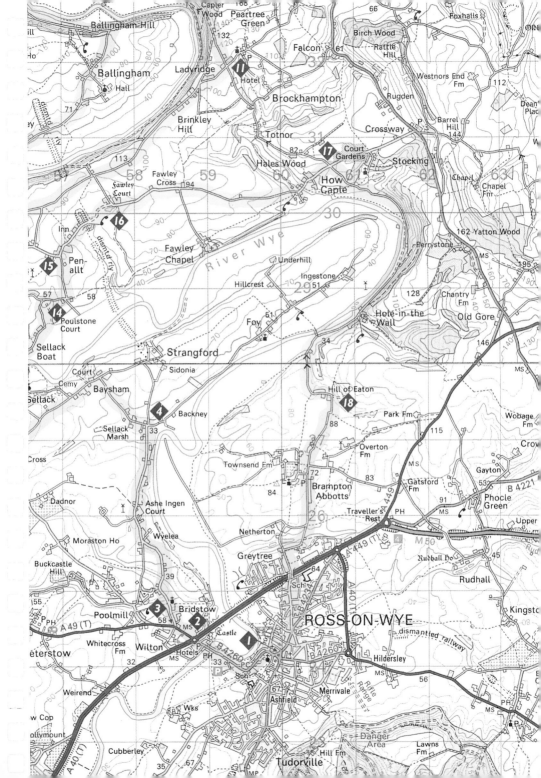

6 Follow signs for Hoarwithy past the Loughpool PH. In Hoarwithy 1st R after New Harp Inn 'King's Caple 1, Carey 1½', then 1st L 'Carey, Ballingham' (**or**, for a short ride, do not turn left but go SA, cross the river and take the 1st R rejoining route at instruction 13)

7 Past the Cottage of Content PH. Climb steadily with reward of spectacular river views after the brow of the hill. Long descent. At T-j R 'Holme Lacy, Hereford'

8 At T-j with B4339 by triangle of grass and horse-chestnut tree R 'Mordiford, Fownhope'

9 After crossing bridge, at T-j with B4224 R 'Ross 11, Fownhope 1½'

10 In Fownhope by the church R 'Capler'. Up, down then the killer hill!

11 At X-roads R 'Hoarwithy'
(For shorter route, SA at X-roads 'How Caple, Foy'. Rejoin route at instruction 17, going SA at X-roads)

12 At T-j R (NS) then 1st L by junction of telephone wires 'Ruxton'

13 At X-roads just past church in King's Caple R 'Sellack Boat'

14 At T-j by triangle of grass with the drive to Poulstone Court to your right turn R (NS)

15 At T-j by triangle of grass and large red barn R 'How Caple'

16 At T-j with lovely red sandstone house ahead R 'How Caple, Ross on Wye, Ledbury'

17 **Easy to miss.** After 2 miles at X-roads (your priority) R 'Ross on Wye'

◀ **page 56**

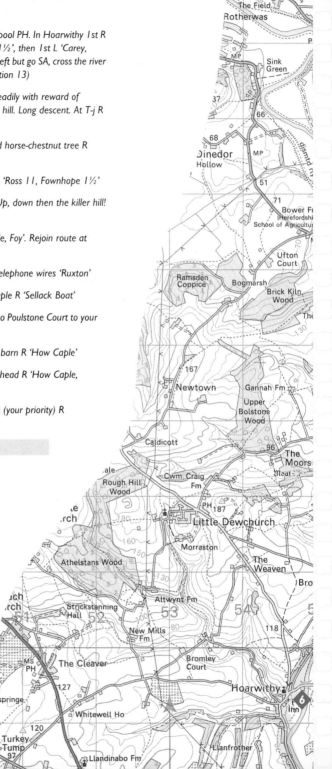

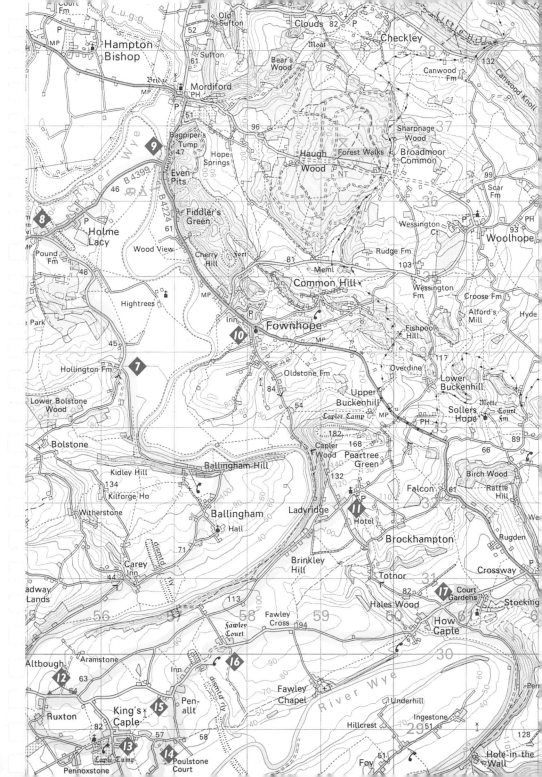

◆ *Beneath the Malverns, west of Upton upon Severn*

A very pleasant, easy ride to the west of the River Severn. The route starts in the attractive old town of Upton upon Severn and drops right down to the banks of the Severn at Ashleworth, famous for its enormous tithe barn. The ride meanders through Highleadon and Upleadon, heading for the splendidly named Redmarley D'Abitot. It passes close to the southern end of the Malverns before returning eastwards to Upton.

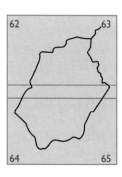

62 | 63

64 | 65

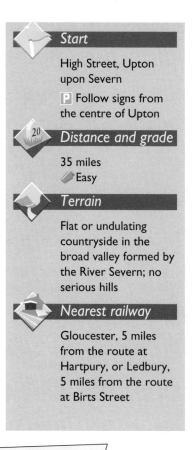

Start

High Street, Upton upon Severn

P Follow signs from the centre of Upton

Distance and grade

35 miles

Easy

Terrain

Flat or undulating countryside in the broad valley formed by the River Severn; no serious hills

Nearest railway

Gloucester, 5 miles from the route at Hartpury, or Ledbury, 5 miles from the route at Birts Street

Refreshments

Several good pubs and teashops in **Upton upon Severn**
Hunters Inn ●●, **Longdon**
Boat Inn ●●, **Ashleworth Quay**
The Arkle PH, **Ashleworth**
Rose and Crown PH ●, **Playley Green**
Duke of York PH ●●, **Rye Street** *(just off the route between instructions 18 and 19)*
Farmers Arms PH ●●, **Birts Street**
Drum and Monkey PH, **Longdon Heath**

Upton upon Severn

Forthampton

Ashleworth

Hartpury

Upton upon Severn 1

An attractive town on the River Severn with some fine inns and a marina. Midsummer Weavers in London Lane is a craft weaving workshop with local products for sale.

Ashleworth Tithe Barn 11

A 15th-century tithe barn with two projecting porch bays and fine roof timbers with queen posts.

Birtsmorton Waterfowl Sanctary 18

Off the route just past instruction 18, the bird sanctuary is set in seven acres and has eighty species of waterfowl plus eagle owls, bustards and barn owls.

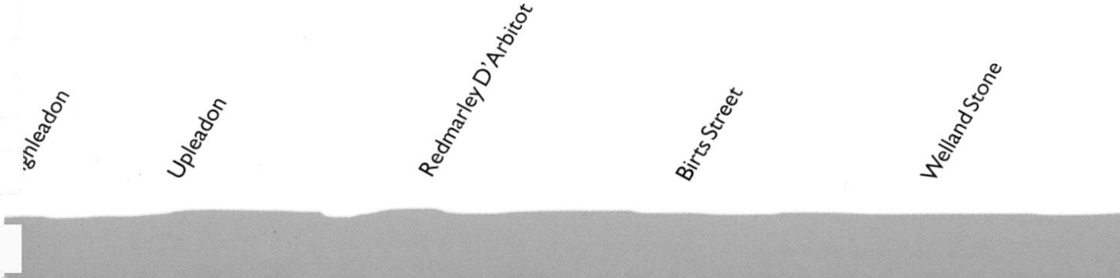

ghleadon

Upleadon

Redmarley D'Arbirot

Birts Street

Welland Stone

1 From Upton take the A4104 away from the river, heading west towards Little Malvern

2 Ignore left turn to Industrial Estate. Climb gentle hill and take next L on B4211 'Gloucester 15¼'

3 Follow this road through Longdon Heath and Longdon. Soon after going under the M50 1st L 'Pipers End, Gullers End, The Rampings'

4 After 2 miles at T-j at the end of The Rampings R 'Tewkesbury, Ledbury', then at T-j with A438 L 'Tewkesbury' and 1st R 'Forthampton 1'

5 At X-roads L 'Lower Lode, Chaceley, Tirley'. Keep following signs for Chaceley and Gloucester

➡ **page 65**

16 At X-roads/sharp RH bend in Redmarley village SA onto Drury Lane 'Unsuitable for Heavy Vehicles'

17 At T-j with A417 L then 1st R 'The Malverns'

18 At T-j with B4208 L 'Tewkesbury 9, Malvern 8'

19 After 1 mile 2nd R 'Birts Street, Birtsmorton'

20 After ¾ mile, with The Farmers Arms PH ahead, bear L 'Castlemorton 1, Upton upon Severn 6'

21 At T-j by church in Castlemorton R (NS)

22 At T-j R 'Longdon Heath 3, Upton upon Severn'

23 Keep following signs for Longdon Heath, ignoring a left turn to Upton upon Severn.

24 At T-j with B4211 L 'Upton upon Severn, Worcester'

25 At T-j with A4104 R 'Upton 1' to return to start

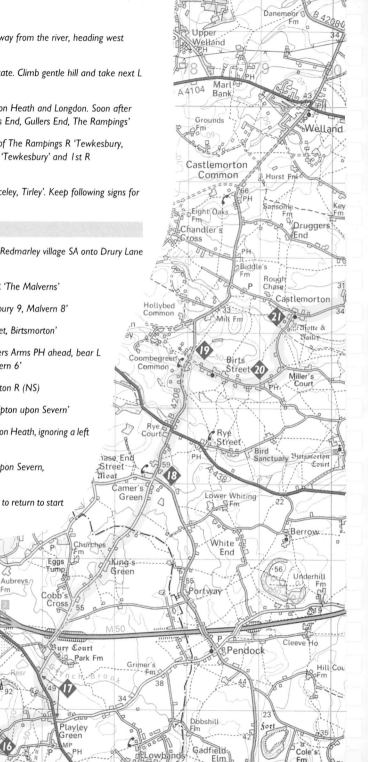

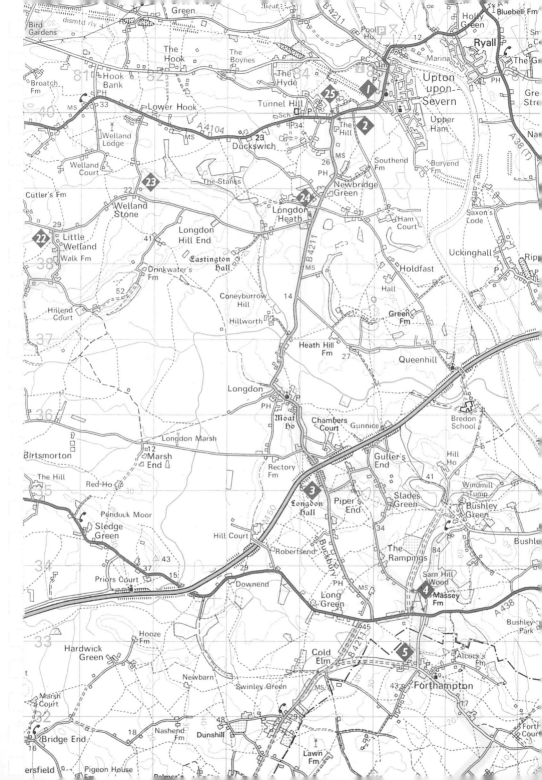

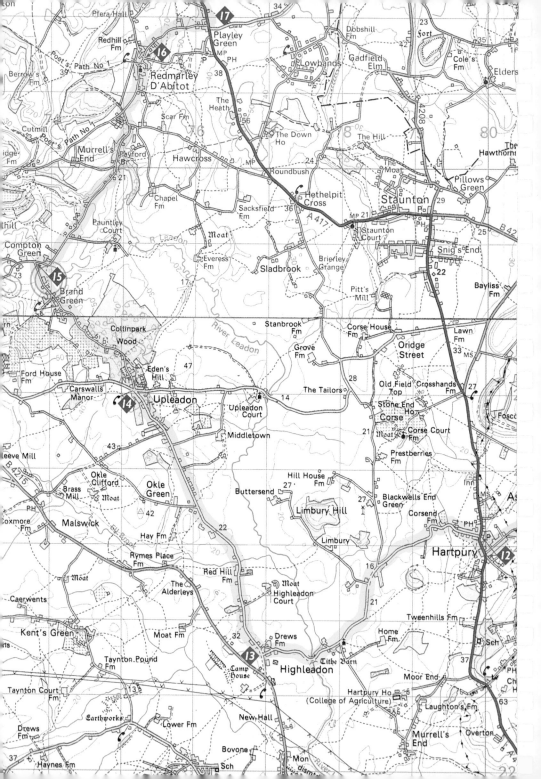

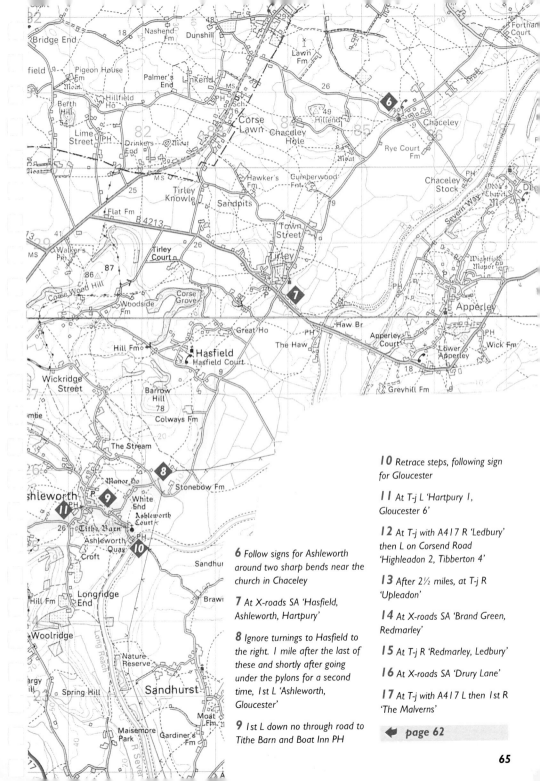

6 Follow signs for Ashleworth around two sharp bends near the church in Chaceley

7 At X-roads SA 'Hasfield, Ashleworth, Hartpury'

8 Ignore turnings to Hasfield to the right. 1 mile after the last of these and shortly after going under the pylons for a second time, 1st L 'Ashleworth, Gloucester'

9 1st L down no through road to Tithe Barn and Boat Inn PH

10 Retrace steps, following sign for Gloucester

11 At T-j L 'Hartpury 1, Gloucester 6'

12 At T-j with A417 R 'Ledbury' then L on Corsend Road 'Highleadon 2, Tibberton 4'

13 After 2½ miles, at T-j R 'Upleadon'

14 At X-roads SA 'Brand Green, Redmarley'

15 At T-j R 'Redmarley, Ledbury'

16 At X-roads SA 'Drury Lane'

17 At T-j with A417 L then 1st R 'The Malverns'

← page 62

Dodging the hills east of Tewkesbury

For such a flat ride this route has a wonderful feeling of being near hills, with the interesting views one associates with harder rides. The route heads for the 'pass' between Oxenton Hill and Nottingham Hill near Gotherington, skirts the lower slopes of the Cotswolds from Gretton to the delightful town of Winchcombe, goes north through Stanway and Stanton, then does a tour of the eastern and southern sides of Bredon Hill. Every now and then there are glimpses of the Malverns to the west. The ride passes through many delightful villages, most notably Stanton and Stanway, but also Elmley Castle, Conderton and Overbury, beneath Bredon Hill. There are plenty of tea shops and pubs along the route.

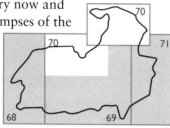

Start

High Street, Tewkesbury

P Follow signs for 'Parking, Swimming Pool' from the centre of Tewkesbury

Distance and grade

38 miles (also shorter routes)

Easy

Terrain

Essentially flat, with two gentle 150-foot climbs

Nearest railway

Evesham, 3 miles from the route at Hinton Cross

Refreshments

The Bugatti, Royal Oak PH 🍴🍴, **Gretton**
Plaisters Arms PH 🍴, Corner Cupboard PH 🍴, plenty of choice, **Winchcombe**
Mount Inn 🍴🍴, **Stanton**
Queen Elisabeth PH 🍴, Old Mill Inn, **Elmley Castle**
Star Inn 🍴, **Ashton under Hill**
Beckford Inn 🍴, coffee shop, **Beckford**
Yew Tree PH, coffee shop **Conderton**
Crown Inn PH 🍴, **Kemerton**

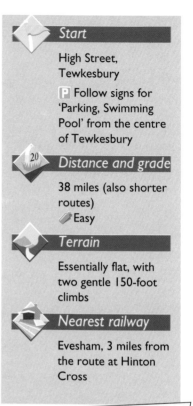

Tewkesbury   Tredington   Gotherington   Gretton   Winchcombe   Stanway   Stanton

Tewkesbury 1
Standing at the confluence of the rivers Severn and Avon, Tewkesbury was an important medieval town. There remains a fascinating maze of small alleyways, half-timbered buildings with overhanging eaves and historic inns. The town is dominated by the magnificent 12th-century abbey church that has the largest Norman tower in existence.

The John Moore Countryside Museum, Church Street, Tewkesbury 1
A countryside collection commemorating the work of John Moore the local naturalist and writer. Ideal for children.

Tewkesbury Town Museum 1
Timber-framed medieval building with social history displays relating to the town and surrounding area, including a reconstructed carpenter's workshop and a model of the Battle of Tewkesbury, one of the bloodiest battles in the Wars of the Roses.

The Little Museum, Tewkesbury 1
15th-century timber-framed house showing the construction of a merchant's shop and house in medieval times.

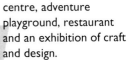

Sudeley Castle, Winchcombe 8
This castle has royal connections going back to the 10th century. Once the property of Ethelred the Unready it later became the palace of Queen Katherine Parr who is buried in the Chapel. There is a shop, plant centre, adventure playground, restaurant and an exhibition of craft and design.

Hailes Abbey 9
Situated southeast of the route at direction 9 in attractive wooded pastureland. The remaining parts of the cloisters and the foundations show the extent of the 13th-century Cistercian abbey.

Stanway House 10
Built of golden limestone in the days of Elizabeth I, Stanway House has a 14th-century tithe barn, a Jacobean gatehouse, collections of unusual furniture and extensive landscaped grounds.

Beckford Silk Printing Centre 21
Silk printing centre specialising in the design, printing and making of silk scarves, ties and other garments. Workshop areas open for viewing, shop and coffee shop.

Conderton Pottery *after 21*
Distinctive stoneware pottery crafted and for sale at the Old Forge, Conderton.

▲ *Winchcombe*

Blake's Hill · Elmley Castle · Ashton under Hill · Beckford · Conderton · Kemerton · Bredon

1 Follow the A438 out of Tewkesbury towards the M5 and Stow-on-the-Wold. Use the cyclepath on the southern side of the road

2 Where cycle track diverts around a red-brick building R onto lane 'Walton Cardiff'. Follow signs for Tredington

3 At T-j R 'Tredington ¾

4 At next T-j L 'Stoke Orchard 1¼, Bishop's Cleeve', then after 300 yards, 1st L 'Gotherington 3½'

5 After the railway crossing 1st R 'Gotherington'

6 At X-roads with A435 SA onto Malleson Road, 'Gotherington ½, Gretton 4'. Follow signs for Gretton and Winchcombe

7 At T-j in Gretton R 'Winchcombe 2½'

8 At T-j in Winchcombe, at the end of North Street L (NS)

➡ **page 70**

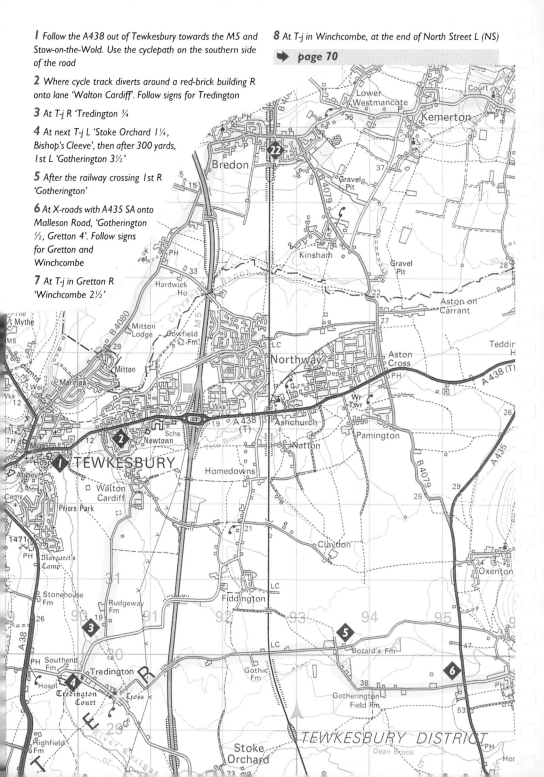

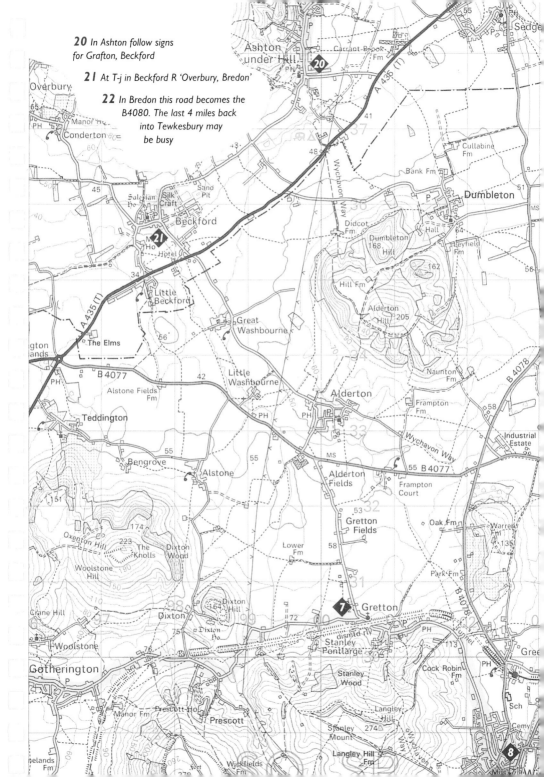

20 In Ashton follow signs
for Grafton, Beckford

21 At T-j in Beckford R 'Overbury, Bredon'

22 In Bredon this road becomes the
B4080. The last 4 miles back
into Tewkesbury may
be busy

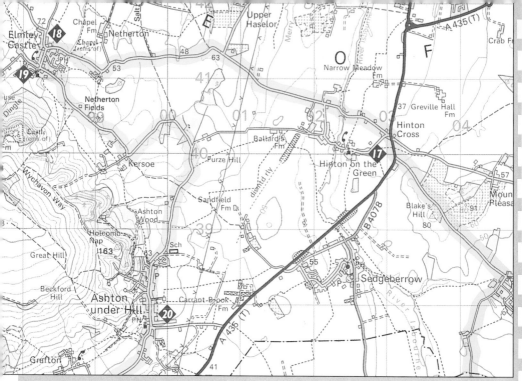

8 At T-j in Winchcombe, at the end of North Street L (NS)

9 After 2 miles (this section may be busy so **take care**), take 2nd of two closely spaced R turns, 'Didbrook'

10 At X-roads with B4077 SA 'Stanton 1½, Stanway House'

11 At T-j R 'Stanton ¼'

12 In Stanton R uphill 'Unsuitable for coaches' for a look at this amazing village, a trip to the Mount Inn PH or both. Retrace route

13 At T-j R towards Broadway

14 At T-j with B4632 R 'Stratford'

15 After ½ mile 1st L 'Manor Farm, Wormington'

16 After 2¼ miles on sharp LH bend at start of Wormington R 'Aston Somerville 1½, Evesham 5'

17 At T-j with A435 R 'Evesham' then 1st L 'Hinton, Elmley Castle'

18 At T-j in Elmley Castle L 'Kerscoe, Ashton under Hill'

19 At end of main street, opposite Elizabeth PH, L 'Kerscoe, Ashton under Hill'

20 In Ashton follow signs for Grafton, Beckford

← **page 69**

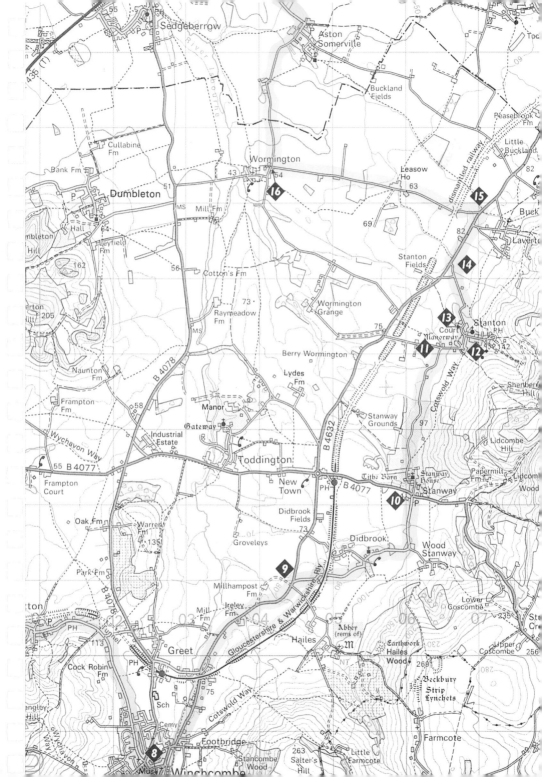

The northern Cotswolds, from Stow-on-the-Wold to Moreton-in-Marsh and Chipping Campden

A tour of the northern end of the Cotswolds, this ride includes visits to the major attractions of Moreton-in-Marsh and Chipping Campden. The second half of the ride passes the highest point on the Cotswolds, with some great views from near Broadway Tower if the weather is favourable. Just when you thought you would never find anywhere to stop for tea, you come upon the Cotswold Farm Park. Stock up with energy for that last unforgiving climb back to Stow from Lower Swell!

76	77
74	75

Refreshments

Plenty of choice in **Stow-on-the-Wold**
Fox PH ♥, **Broadwell**
Churchill PH ♥, **Paxford**
Black Bear PH ♥, plenty of choice in
Moreton-in-Marsh
Kings Arms PH ♥, Noel Arms PH ♥ ♥,
plenty of choice in **Chipping Campden**

Start

Tourist Information Centre, Stow-on-the-Wold

P Long-stay car park on the A436 Chipping Norton road out of Stow

Distance and grade

31 miles

//// Moderate

Terrain

Stow is on a hill, Moreton-in-Marsh and Chipping Campden are in dips and south of Broadway Tower is the highest point in the Cotswolds (1083 feet). Four climbs: 230 feet from Moreton to Batsford, 580 feet from Chipping Campden to Broadway Tower, 200 feet between Chalk Hill and Swell Hill Farm and then 280 feet up from Lower Swell.

Nearest railway

Moreton-in-Marsh

Stow-on-the-Wold Broadwell Evenlode Moreton-in-Marsh Batsford Aston Magna Paxford Chipping Campden

Stow-on-the-Wold 1

This is the highest hilltop town in the Cotswolds lying on a ridge between the upper valleys of the rivers Windrush and Evenlode. The focal point of the town is the 14th-century cross situated in the market square.

Moreton-in-Marsh 6

The main street of this town is formed by the Roman Fosse Way

Batsford Park Arboretum 9

One of the largest private collections of trees in the country in over 50 acres of garden with bronze statues from the Orient, a garden centre and nursery.

Falconry Centre, Batsford Park 9

Located adjacent to Batsford Arboretum, there is a collection of over 70 birds of prey with flying demonstrations of eagles, owls, hawks and falcons.

Woolstaplers Hall Museum, Chipping Campden 13

The Hall was constructed in 1340 for merchants to buy the staples of Cotswold fleece and is now a museum housing a collection of town and country bygones.

▲ *Almshouses, Chipping Campden*

Broadway Tower Country Park 15/16

On a clear day there are breathtaking views over 12 counties from Broadway Tower, built in the late 1700s by the Earl of Coventry. Facilities within the Country Park include picnic areas, a children's farmyard, animal enclosures, an adventure playground and a restaurant

Cotswold Farm Park 18/19

The most comprehensive collection of rare breeds of British farm animals in the country, and the premier rare breed and survival centre. Events such as lambing, milking and shearing can be seen at certain times of the year and there are special weekends such as the wool, wood and blacksmith weekends.

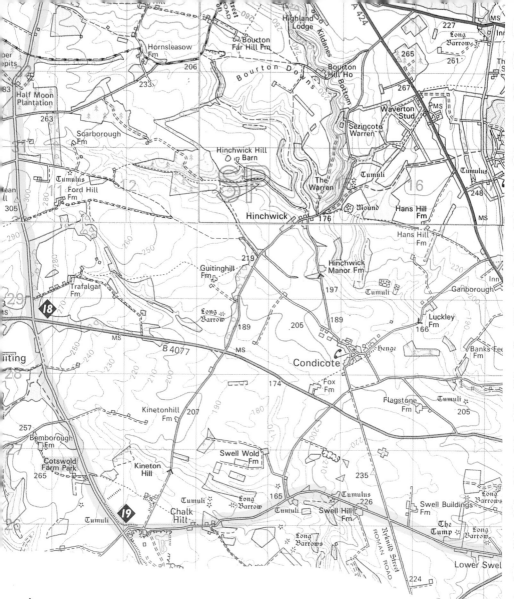

1 With your back to the Tourist Information Centre, turn R past the antiques shop and White Hart PH towards the Stratford road

2 At T-j with A429 R 'Stratford' through traffic lights

3 After ¼ mile 1st R 'Broadwell 1¼, Evenlode 3'

4 At T-j at the bottom of the hill R 'Evenlode 2, Oddington 2'. At 2nd T-j R again (same sign)

5 After 200 yards 1st L 'Evenlode 2, Adlestrop 3'

6 After 5 miles, in Moreton-in-Marsh at T-j with A44 L 'Evesham'

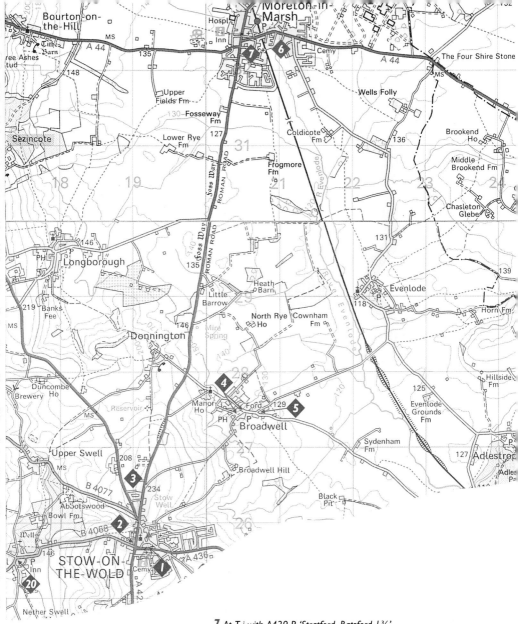

7 At T-j with A429 R 'Stratford, Batsford 1¾'

➡ **page 77**

18 At X-roads with B4077 SA 'The Slaughters, Bourton'
(Good tea stop at Cotswold Farm Park from April to September)

19 At 1st X-roads after Cotswold Farm Park L (sign broken)

20 At T-j with B4068 L 'Stow 1'. At traffic lights in Stow SA 'Car and coach park', then 1st L 'Town centre, light vehicles only'

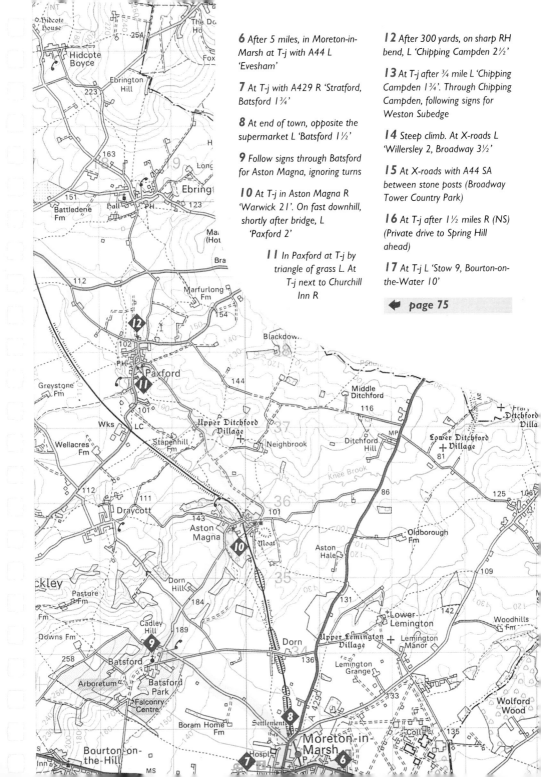

6 *After 5 miles, in Moreton-in-Marsh at T-j with A44 L 'Evesham'*

7 *At T-j with A429 R 'Stratford, Batsford 1¾'*

8 *At end of town, opposite the supermarket L 'Batsford 1½'*

9 *Follow signs through Batsford for Aston Magna, ignoring turns*

10 *At T-j in Aston Magna R 'Warwick 21'. On fast downhill, shortly after bridge, L 'Paxford 2'*

11 *In Paxford at T-j by triangle of grass L. At T-j next to Churchill Inn R*

12 *After 300 yards, on sharp RH bend, L 'Chipping Campden 2½'*

13 *At T-j after ¾ mile L 'Chipping Campden 1¾'. Through Chipping Campden, following signs for Weston Subedge*

14 *Steep climb. At X-roads L 'Willersley 2, Broadway 3½'*

15 *At X-roads with A44 SA between stone posts (Broadway Tower Country Park)*

16 *At T-j after 1½ miles R (NS) (Private drive to Spring Hill ahead)*

17 *At T-j L 'Stow 9, Bourton-on-the-Water 10'*

← page 75

South from Stow-on-the-Wold to the Windrush Valley and Northleach

The ride links together some very attractive Cotswold villages, most notably Northleach, Lower Slaughter and Bourton-on-the-Water. The latter attracts thousands of people every year and is probably best appreciated by bike as you are unlikely to get caught up in the coach jams. The route also takes you to the less well-known villages of Icomb and Sherborne. The first half of the ride passes few refreshment facilities but both Northleach and Bourton-on-the-Water have more than enough to make up for this.

Refreshments

Plenty of choice in **Stow-on-the-Wold**
Lamb PH ✿✿, **Great Rissington** *(just off the route)*
Red Lion PH ✿, *Wheatsheaf PH* ✿, *plenty of choice in* **Northleach**
Plenty of choice in **Bourton-on-the-Water** *(likely to be full of coaches)*
Fox Inn ✿, **Great Barrington**

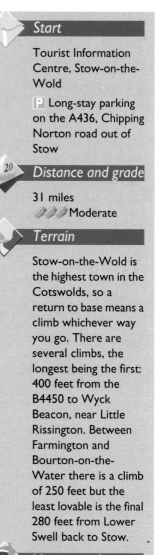

Start

Tourist Information Centre, Stow-on-the-Wold

P Long-stay parking on the A436, Chipping Norton road out of Stow

Distance and grade

31 miles
Moderate

Terrain

Stow-on-the-Wold is the highest town in the Cotswolds, so a return to base means a climb whichever way you go. There are several climbs, the longest being the first: 400 feet from the B4450 to Wyck Beacon, near Little Rissington. Between Farmington and Bourton-on-the-Water there is a climb of 250 feet but the least lovable is the final 280 feet from Lower Swell back to Stow.

Nearest railway

Kingham, 3 miles east of Icomb

78

Bourton-on-the-Water 17

Graceful low bridges span the river Windrush at Bourton-on-the-Water and the village is often described as 'The Venice of the Cotswolds'. At its centre there is a church with a 14th-century chancel and a domed Georgian tower. There are many other places of interest in Bourton-on-the-Water:

Model Village

Located in the High Street, this model was built in 1937 in local stone 1/9th the size of the real village.

Folly Farm Waterfowl

Over 160 breeds of waterfowl, wildfowl, ducks and geese in natural habitats on ponds and lakes. Also an extensive garden centre and tea rooms.

Model Railway

Some of the finest operating scenic model railway layouts in the country with over forty British and continental trains. There is a large shop with quality toys, models, trains and accessories.

Birdland

Situated on the river Windrush, Birdland has one of the most interesting collections of endangered species in the world. The penguin rookery has a glass front so they can be viewed underwater.

Cotswold Motor Museum

Located in an 18th-century watermill there are cars, motorcycles, over 800 vintage advertising signs, a display of 1920s caravans and vintage pedal cars and toys.

Cotswold Countryside Collection, Northleach

Cotswold rural life and tradition displayed in a prison with a restored cell block and courtroom.

Northleach   Farmington   Bourton-on-the-Water   Lower Slaughter   Lower Swell

1 From the Tourist Information Centre head out of town past the King's Arms PH and the bank on the one-way street. At T-j with A436 L 'Chipping Norton'

2 After ¾ mile R on B4450, 'Bledington 3, Kingham 5'

3 After 1¼ miles, at bottom of hill, immediately after crossing a hump-backed bridge R 'Icomb 1½'. **Take care**

4 At T-j by triangle of grass and memorial stone in Icomb R (NS) and climb hill

5 At T-j L 'Little Rissington 3, Burford 8'

6 At T-j with A424 SA (NS) passing airfield

➡ **page 83**

16 After 2½ miles at T-j bear L 'Bourton 2, Stow 6'

17 Bear R at triangle of grass on the lower road (your priority). In Bourton-on-the-Water, at X-roads near woollens shop L (NS)

18 At T-j with A429 R 'Stow', then L 'Naunton 4'

19 Shortly 1st R 'Lower Slaughter 1, Upper Slaughter 1½'

20 After ¾ mile 1st R downhill. At T-j by stream in Lower Slaughter R (NS)

21 Cross bridge. At T-j by triangle of grass with church ahead L (NS)

22 At T-j with B4068 in Lower Swell R 'Stow 1'

23 At traffic lights in Stow SA 'Car and Coach Park', then 1st L 'Town centre, light vehicles only'

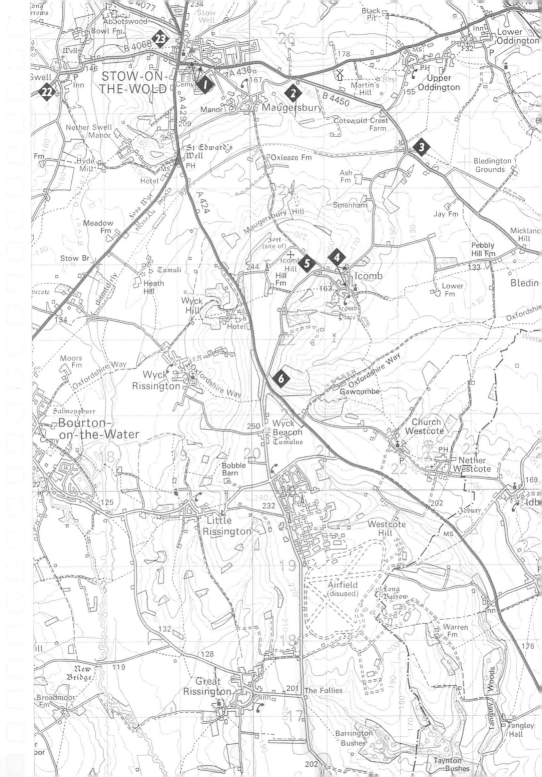

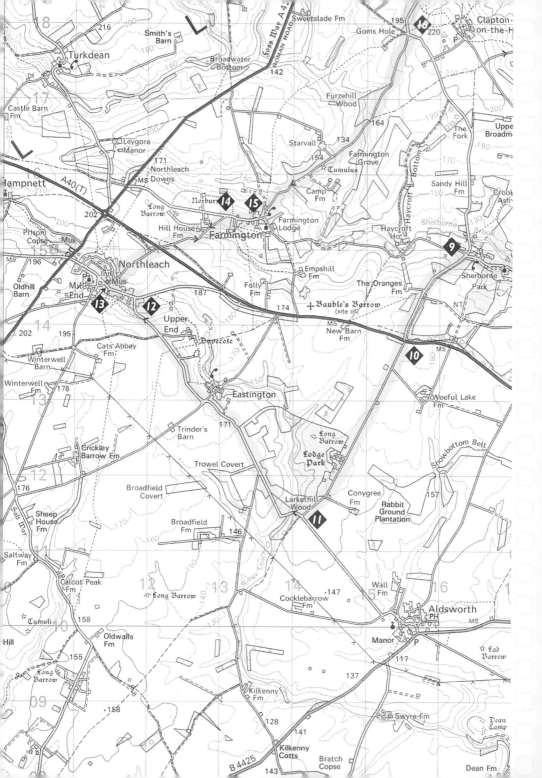

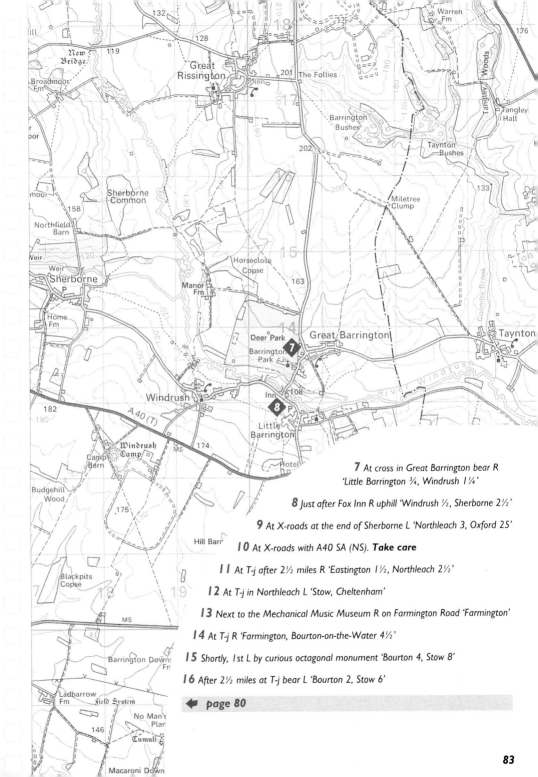

7 At cross in Great Barrington bear R 'Little Barrington ¾, Windrush 1¼'

8 Just after Fox Inn R uphill 'Windrush ½, Sherborne 2½'

9 At X-roads at the end of Sherborne L 'Northleach 3, Oxford 25'

10 At X-roads with A40 SA (NS). **Take care**

11 At T-j after 2½ miles R 'Eastington 1½, Northleach 2½'

12 At T-j in Northleach L 'Stow, Cheltenham'

13 Next to the Mechanical Music Museum R on Farmington Road 'Farmington'

14 At T-j R 'Farmington, Bourton-on-the-Water 4½'

15 Shortly, 1st L by curious octagonal monument 'Bourton 4, Stow 8'

16 After 2½ miles at T-j bear L 'Bourton 2, Stow 6'

◀ page 80

From Cirencester along the edge of the Golden Valley and on to Withington

The numerous straight roads emanating from Cirencester are evidence of the fact that it once was a Roman town, Corinium. In general, these are now main roads and of little interest to the cyclist. The route heads south from here, then west to the very edge of the Golden Valley along which the River Frome and the Stroudwater Canal run. There are superb views from between Frampton Mansell and Sapperton. Easy riding takes you north through the villages of Winstone and Elkstone before you encounter the hills and valleys formed by the River Churn,

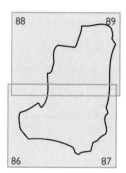

Hilcot Brook and the River Coln at Withington. One last climb takes you to the top of the ridge where you feel as though you are on the roof of the Cotswolds as you begin your long, gentle descent back into Cirencester.

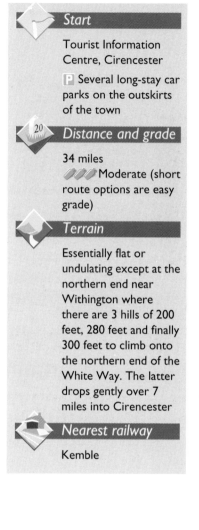

Start

Tourist Information Centre, Cirencester

P Several long-stay car parks on the outskirts of the town

Distance and grade

34 miles

🚴🚴🚴 Moderate (short route options are easy grade)

Terrain

Essentially flat or undulating except at the northern end near Withington where there are 3 hills of 200 feet, 280 feet and finally 300 feet to climb onto the northern end of the White Way. The latter drops gently over 7 miles into Cirencester

Nearest railway

Kemble

Cirencester · Ewen · Tarlton · Frampton Mansell · Sapperton

Cirencester 1

Corinium Dobunorum was the name of this Roman town that became the second largest in England. When the Romans withdrew, Cirencester declined but its strategic position at the confluence of the major routeways, Fosse Way, Ermin Way and Akeman Street, combined with its vast sheep pastures brought it

▼ Cirencester

great wealth in the Middle Ages. Money from the wool paid for the Church of St John the Baptist, one of the largest of its kind in the country. Other places of interest in the town are:

Corinium Museum

An impressive collection of Roman remains clearly displayed to relate to the development of the Cotswolds from the earliest times with special reference to the Roman period.

Cirencester Workshops

Located at Brewery Court in the town this Victorian brewery has been converted and houses a range of craft workshops including leatherworkers, textiles, bookbinders and a blacksmith. There is a gallery showing exhibitions and a wholefood coffee house.

Duntisbourne Abbots 14

This village stands at the head of a beautiful wooded valley.

Refreshments

Slug & Lettuce PH🦆, plenty of choice in **Cirencester**   Wild Duck PH🦆🦆, **Ewen** Thames Head PH🦆, **Kemble** (just east of instruction 8)   Tunnel House PH🦆🦆, just north of **Tarlton** (instruction 9) Crown PH🦆, **Frampton Mansell** Bell PH🦆🦆, **Sapperton** Colesbourne Inn🦆, **Colesbourne** The Mill PH🦆, **Withington**

Miserden Park 14

Shrubs, roses, perennial borders, topiary and spring bulbs in a picturesque woodland setting.

Withington 22

A pretty village in the Coln Valley that has an unusually large church as its focal point.

Winstone   Elkstone   Withington   White Way

1 With your back to the Tourist Information Centre L towards church, then at traffic lights L on Cricklade Street. You have the right to cycle along this pedestrianised street but it may be busy so show consideration

2 At next traffic lights R on Querns Lane, then at T-j with more major road L

3 At X-roads SA onto Somerford Road

4 At next T-j R 'Somerford Keynes'

5 Ignore a turning on the left to Siddington and take next R by a large oak tree 'Ewen 2, Kemble 3', following signs for Kemble and Tarlton

6 At T-j in Ewen R 'Kemble 1, Tarlton 3½'

7 At X-roads SA 'Kemble Station, Tarlton 2½'. At X-roads with A429 SA (same sign)

8 At X-roads with A433 SA (NS)

9 Through Tarlton following signs for Rodmarton, then at the end of the village, opposite the water tower R 'Cherington 4'

10 At T-j R 'Frampton Mansell', following road round a sharp RH bend and signs for Frampton Mansell

11 At X-roads with A419 SA 'Frampton Mansell'

12 Follow signs for Sapperton. At X-roads SA 'Sapperton Village'

13 At T-j L 'Daglingworth 3¼, Duntisbourne 4'. Follow signs for Winstone (For short alternative after 1½ miles, R 'Daglingworth')

➡ **page 88**

25 At traffic lights with A417 SA. Follow one-way system along Spitalgate Lane and Dollar Street back to church, market place and Tourist Information Centre

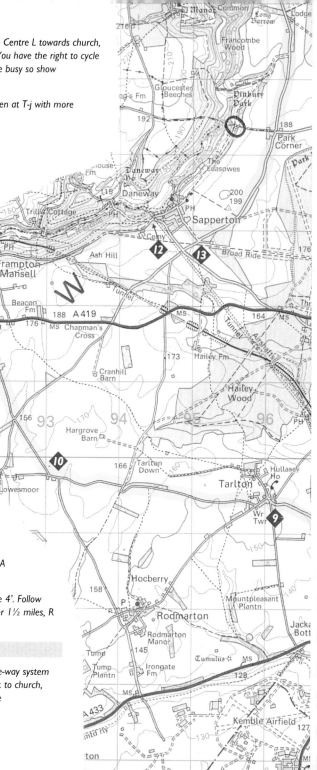

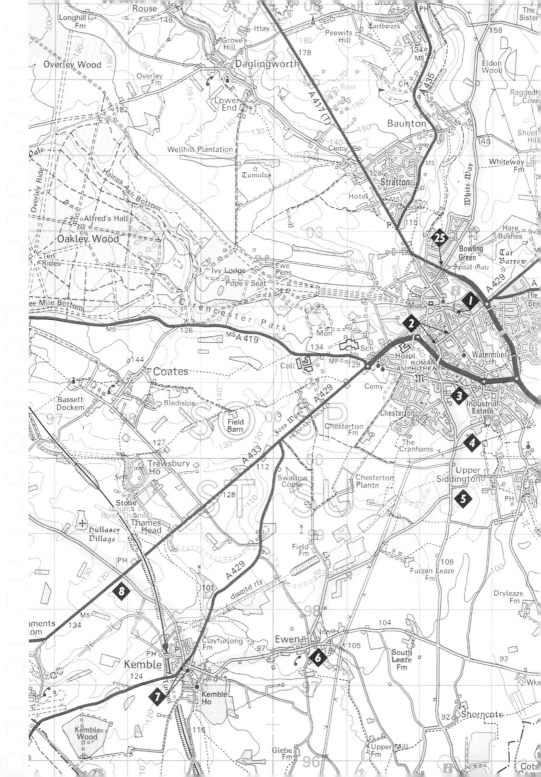

14 In Winstone follow signs for Elkstone, turning L at X-roads (your priority) onto Pike Road 'Elkstone 2, Birdlip 4'

15 At X-roads with A417 SA 'Elkstone, Cowley'

16 At X-roads with telephone box SA 'Cowley ½, Cheltenham 6'. At **next** X-roads just before road starts to descend R 'Colesbourne 2, Woodmancote 4'

17 After 1½ miles at X-roads beneath pylons L 'Colesbourne 1, Cheltenham 7' (For short alternative at X-roads SA 'Woodmancote 2½, Cirencester 8')

18 At bottom of hill, by triangle of grass L 'Hilcot 2, Cheltenham 6'

19 At T-j with A435 R 'Cirencester', then L 'Hilcot 1¾'

20 At X-roads R 'Withington 2'

21 At T-j L 'Withington ¼, Chedworth 3½'

22 In Withington at junction SA 'Andoversford 3, Cheltenham 8½'. After 200 yards at T-j R 'Roman Villa 2¾, Compton Abdale 2¼'

23 1st R after Mill Inn PH on Woodbridge Lane 'Unsuitable for Heavy Vehicles'

24 At T-j L (NS). Climb through wood to top of ridge and follow for 7 miles towards Cirencester

← page 86

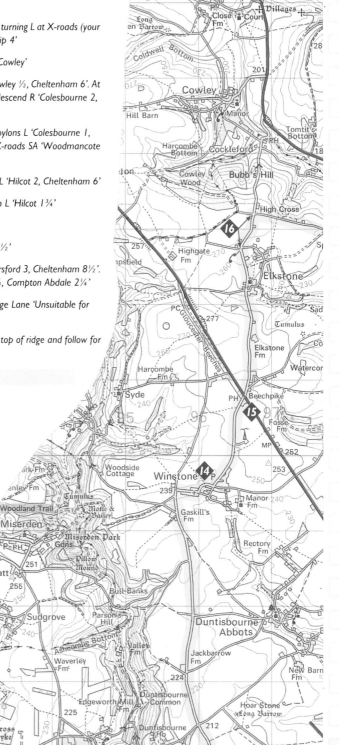

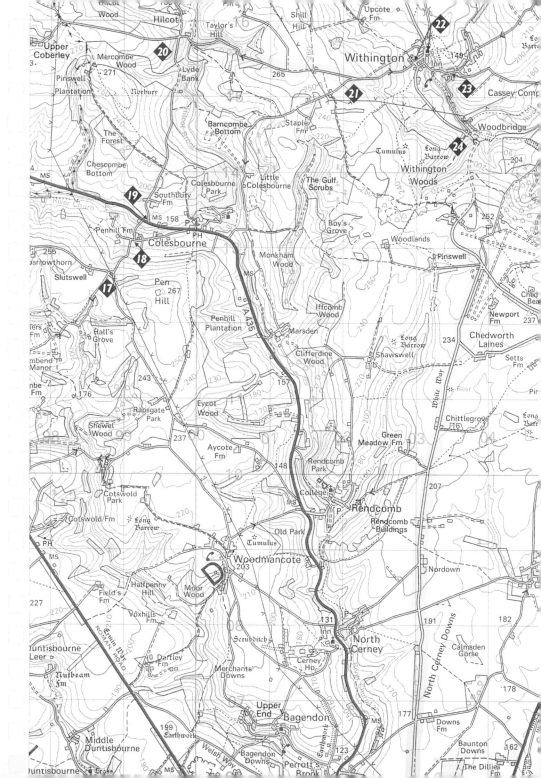

13 Very easy riding in the Severn Vale around Frampton on Severn

Start

The Green, Frampton on Severn

P Small car park by the post office, Frampton on Severn

Distance and grade

10, 12 and 12 miles (three loops total 34 miles)

Easy

Terrain

Flat

Nearest railway

Stonehouse, 2 miles from the route at Frocester or Gloucester, 4 miles from the route at Elmore

Here is an ideal ride or series of short rides for people who want to start cycling or take it up again. It is also suitable for more experienced cyclists who do not need the challenge of the Cotswold escarpment and simply want to enjoy the quiet lanes and river views of this tucked-away corner of the Severn Vale. Starting from the spacious village of Frampton on Severn, the ride heads westwards right to the banks of the Severn at Arlingham Passage, with fine views across to the Forest of Dean. You would have to travel over 30 miles by road to get to Newnham, the village that is just a few hundred yards away on the other side of the river. Returning eastwards you have a choice of finishing after this first loop of 10 miles and going back to Frampton or heading north and doing the second loop via Longney and Elmore. A detour to the river at Weir Green is worthwhile just to see how much smaller it has become in a few miles. The third loop crosses to the other side of the M5 as far as Frocester, with the Cotswolds looming ahead, before returning via Cambridge and Slimbridge and a short spell on the Gloucester and Sharpness Canal towpath back to Frampton.

The third loop uses a short section of the canal towpath. You will need a permit from the British Waterways Board, Llanthony Warehouse, The Docks, Gloucester GL1 2EJ. Tel: 01452-25524.

Frampton on Severn   Arlingham   Overton   Longney   Elmore

Places of interest

Frampton on Severn

The village green at Frampton on Severn covers more than 20 acres. It is fringed by a number of Georgian houses including Frampton Court which is a grade I Vanbrugh House and family home. Frampton Manor stands at the other side of the green, a timber-framed house with a walled garden that is said to be the birthplace of 'Fair Rosamund' Clifford, a mistress of Henry II.

Refreshments

The Bell PH, **Frampton on Severn**
Red Lion PH, Old Passage Inn, **Arlingham**
The Ship Inn, Saul Anchor Inn, **Epney**
Queen Victoria PH, Kings Head PH, **Eastington**
Royal Gloucestershire Hussars PH, **Frocester**

▲ The Gloucester and Sharpness canal

Longney   Whitminster   Eastington   Frocester   Cambridge

Loop 1

1 From the Bell Inn in Frampton go west towards Saul, Framilode and Arlingham

2 After crossing canal, on sharp RH bend bear L (in effect SA) 'Fretherne, Arlingham 3'. Continue on this road for 3½ miles right to the end at the Old Passage Inn.

3 Retrace the route for 2½ miles. On a small rise, opposite Overton Farm, near a pylon on your left L 'Overton Lane'

4 After a short stretch by the river, at a T-j R (NS)

5 At T-j at the High Street in Saul either R to return to Frampton or L 'Upper Framilode' to continue on 2nd loop

Loop 2

6 After 2½ miles, at T-j in Longney, by Manor Farm L 'Elmore'

7 Go through Elmore. **Easy to miss**. 1 mile after left turn to Stonebench R 'Longney 2, Epney 2'

8 After 2½ miles L by triangle of grass. 'Epney, Saul 2½, Frampton 3½' to rejoin outward route

9 In Saul either SA to return to Frampton or L by the church on Church Lane 'Whitminster 2½' to continue on 3rd loop

Loop 3

10 At T-j L 'Whitminster 1½'

11 At X-roads with A38 SA by Old Forge PH onto Grove Lane 'Westend 1, Nupend 1½'

➡ **page 94**

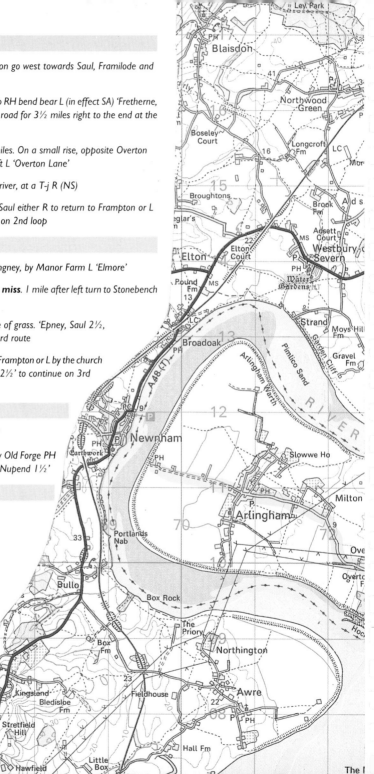

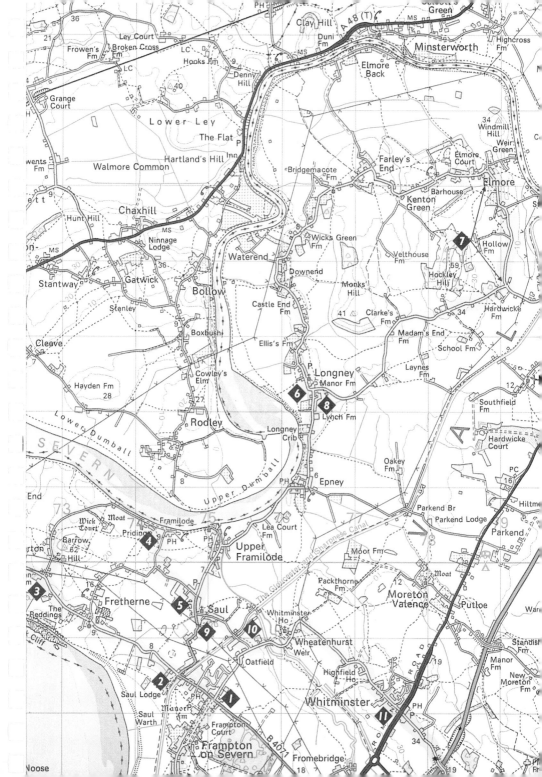

Loop 1

1 From the Bell Inn in Frampton go west towards Saul, Framilode and Arlingham

2 After crossing canal, on sharp RH bend bear L (in effect SA) 'Fretherne, Arlingham 3'. Continue on this road for 3½ miles right to the end at the Old Passage Inn.

3 Retrace the route for 2½ miles. On a small rise, opposite Overton Farm, near a pylon on your left L 'Overton Lane'

4 After a short stretch by the river, at a T-j R (NS)

5 At T-j at the High Street in Saul either R to return to Frampton or L 'Upper Framilode' to continue on 2nd loop at instruction 6

Loop 3

10 At T-j L 'Whitminster 1½'

11 At X-roads with A38 SA by Old Forge PH (NS)

12 At roundabout with A419 SA 'Eastington 1'

13 At roundabout at the end of Eastington L 'Frocester, Bath'

14 At X-roads in Frocester by Royal Gloucestershire Hussars PH R 'Coaley 2, Dursley 6'

15 At T-j shortly after going under railway bridge R 'Cam 3, Dursley 4'

16 400 yards after going under railway bridge a second time, 1st R opposite letter box (NS)

17 At T-j L through lay-by onto A38, then R just past the George Inn onto Ryalls Lane (NS)

18 Follow this SA through 'no through road' sign and over canal bridge

19 R along towpath, recrossing canal at 1st (white) bridge and following road back into Frampton

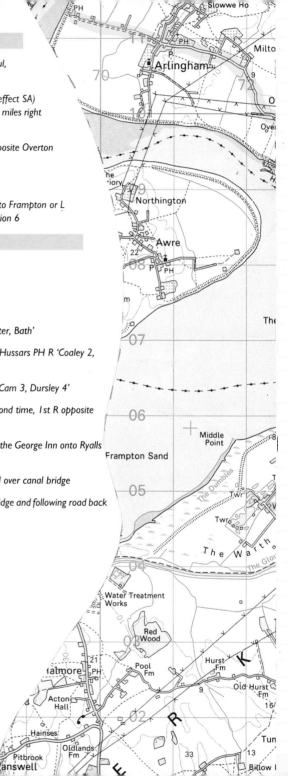

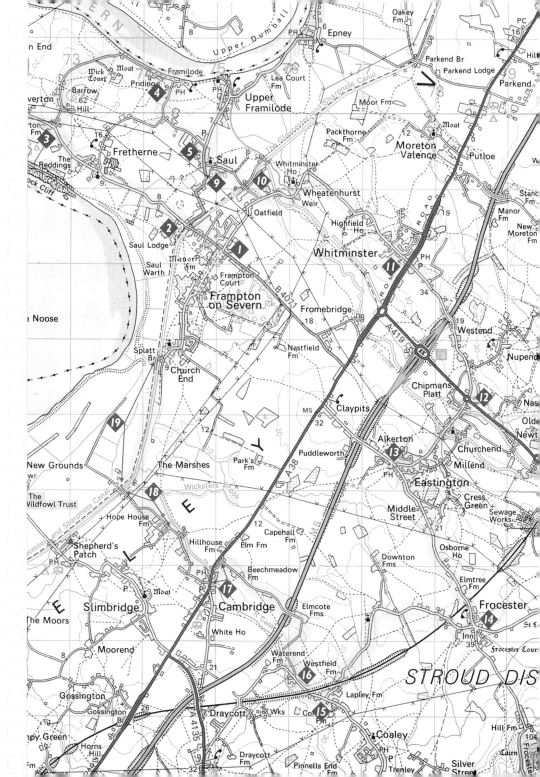

14 From Wotton-under-Edge to the River Severn, returning via Uley

Start

Wotton-under-Edge

P Small car park following signs for Hillesley and Alderley

20 Distance and grade

30 miles

Moderate/strenuous

Terrain

A short, sharp 300-foot climb at the start onto Wotton Hill. Descent to Severn Vale for easy cycling. The climb back onto the Cotswolds is split into two: a gradual then steeper climb from the Vale to Uley; a much longer, steeper hill from Uley to the A4135 (470 feet)

Nearest railway

Stonehouse, 4 miles from Coaley

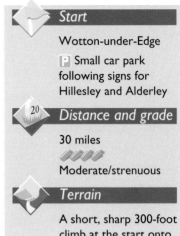

You will find this a ride of contrasts, with some very easy riding in the Vale of Severn and two hard climbs, one at the start and one near the end. The route avoids the busy B4060 north of Wotton by climbing Wotton Hill and dropping via Waterley Bottom to North Nibley, providing wide views out towards the river. Three points of interest in the Vale of Berkeley are Berkeley Castle, the Gloucester and Sharpness Canal and The Wildfowl Trust at Slimbridge. The hills beckon and the route weaves its way between Cam Long Down, Uley Bury and Downham Hill before dropping into Uley. You now face the real test: Bencome Hill, 480 feet of climbing in a mile. The return to Wotton uses a road that is busier than one might normally choose but the rewards are not only magnificent views right at the edge of the escarpment near the golf course but also a thrilling descent back down to the start.

Refreshments

Plenty of choice in **Wotton-under-Edge**
New Inn P●●, **Waterley Bottom** *(just north of instruction 4)* Black Horse PH●, **North Nibley** *Plenty of choice in* **Berkeley** The Salmon PH●, **Wanswell** Berkeley Arms PH●, Berkeley Hunt Inn, **Purton** Tudor Arms PH●, **Shepherd's Patch** *(just west of instruction 18)* Old Crown PH●, **Uley**

Wotton-under-Edge / Wotton Hill — North Nibley — Berkeley — Wanswell — Purton — Halmore

Wotton-under-Edge

A market town with 17th- and 18th-century houses. Isaac Pitman (1813-1897) inventor of shorthand was born in Orchard Street.

Berkeley 11

A quiet Georgian town dominated by the castle, Berkeley also has a fine Early English church which contains many memorials to the Berkeley family. The churchyard contains the grave of Edward Jenner (1749-1823) pioneer of smallpox vaccination who was born here.

▲ Uley Bury

Berkeley Castle 11

Situated south of the town of Berkeley this Norman fortress, built in the reign of Henry II, has been transformed into a magnificent stately home surrounded by Elizabethan terraced gardens. It has been the ancestral home of the Berkeley family for over 800 years. A butterfly farm set in a walled garden houses many species of exotic and British butterflies.

Hetty Pegler's Tump 22

A Neolithic Long Barrow where 38 skeletons have been found. It is 120 by 22 feet with 4 chambers.

Uley Bury 23

This commanding Iron Age fort is a superb vantage point with deep ramparts covering 32 acres.

Slimbridge   Cambridge   Coaley   Uley   A4135

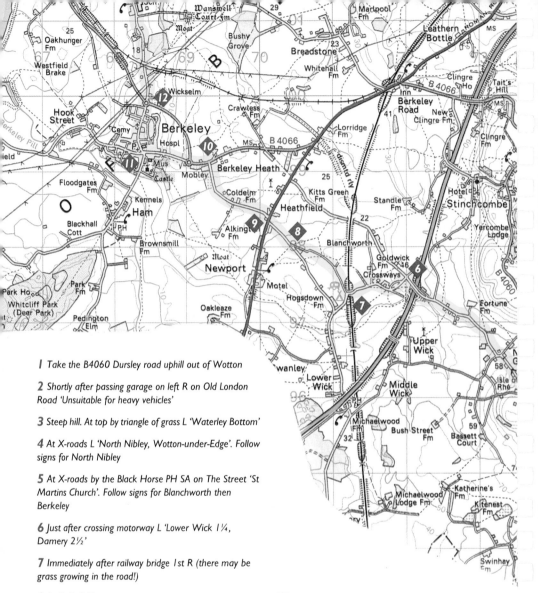

1 *Take the B4060 Dursley road uphill out of Wotton*

2 *Shortly after passing garage on left R on Old London Road 'Unsuitable for heavy vehicles'*

3 *Steep hill. At top by triangle of grass L 'Waterley Bottom'*

4 *At X-roads L 'North Nibley, Wotton-under-Edge'. Follow signs for North Nibley*

5 *At X-roads by the Black Horse PH SA on The Street 'St Martins Church'. Follow signs for Blanchworth then Berkeley*

6 *Just after crossing motorway L 'Lower Wick 1¼, Damery 2½'*

7 *Immediately after railway bridge 1st R (there may be grass growing in the road!)*

8 *At T-j R (NS)*

9 *At T-j with A38 R 'Gloucester', then L 'Sharpness 3½'*

10 *At T-j with B4066 L 'Berkeley ½, Sharpness 4'. At roundabout SA*

11 *In Berkeley follow road round to the R onto Marybrook Street 'Sharpness'*

12 *At roundabout SA 'Wanswell 1'*

➡ **page 100**

22 *Follow road through Coaley and Hamshill. At the end of Far Green, on sharp RH bend, bear L (in effect SA) uphill 'Uley'*

23 *At fork in road bear R down Fop Street 'Dursley'*

24 *At X-roads SA 'Stoutshill, Kingscote 2½, Tetbury 7½'*

25 *Steep climb. At X-roads with B4058 R 'Wotton 3½, Dursley 3½'*

26 *At T-j with A4135 R, then at junction after 400 yards bear L 'Wotton' to return to start via wonderful downhill*

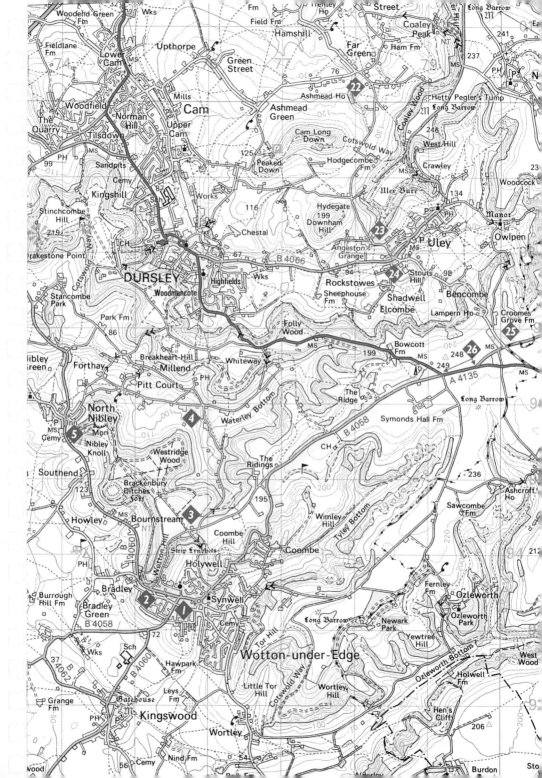

10 *At T-j with B4066 L 'Berkeley ½, Sharpness 4'. At roundabout SA*

11 *In Berkeley follow road round to R onto Marybrook Street 'Sharpness'*

12 *At roundabout SA 'Wanswell 1'*

13 *Shortly after the Salmon Inn PH in Wanswell ignore the 1st right to Halmore and Breadstone. On a sharp LH bend after 150 yards take the next R 'Purton, Brookend'*

14 *In Purton either L over bridge for Berkeley Hunt Inn or Berkeley Arms Inn and river views or follow road around into Halmore*

15 Easy to miss. *At end of Halmore, opposite red-brick Halmore Cottage L 'Gossington, Slimbridge'*

16 Easy to miss. *Shortly after Old Hurst Farm Guest House L on Moorend Lane 'Slimbridge'*

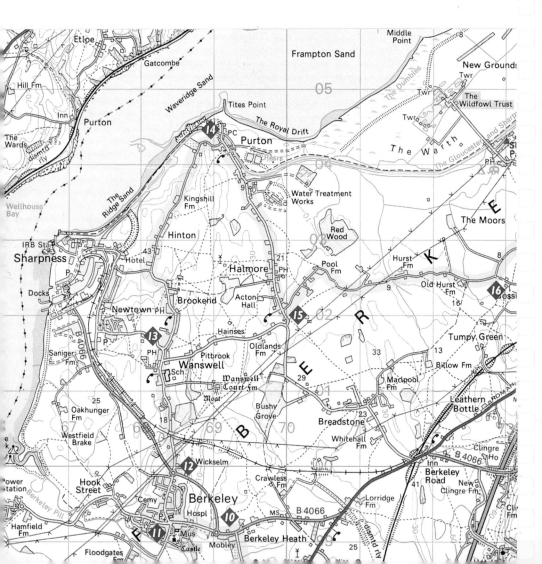

17 At T-j with St John's Road L 'Slimbridge, Severn Wildfowl Trust 1½'

18 At end of Slimbridge opposite long red-brick barn R on Longaston Lane 'Troytown'

19 At T-j with Ryalls Lane R

20 At T-j with A38 L then R just past George PH into lay-by and 1st R

21 At T-j opposite the interesting buildings of Coaley Mill L (NS)

22 Follow road through Coaley and Hamshill. At the end of Far Green, on sharp RH bend bear L (in effect SA) uphill 'Uley'

← **page 98**

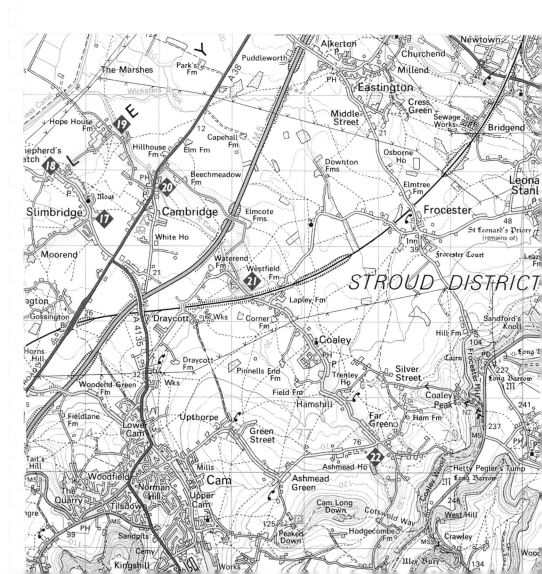

Bredon Hill, north of Tewkesbury

Bredon Hill is a distinctive lump of land northeast of Tewkesbury. Lying in the broad, flat valley of the Severn, its 975-foot summit has magnificent views all around: south to Alderton Hill, Nottingham Hill and Langley Hill; east towards the Cotswold escarpment; west to the Malverns and north across the Vale of Evesham. There are some very attractive villages at the base of the hill and the tracks are, in general, well signposted and well maintained by the Overbury Estate. The ride is made up of two loops, both of which climb the slightly less steep southern side of the hill on tarmac or good solid track almost to the top. There are several other good tracks, particularly on the southern side of the hill, which are not described in this ride and which would enable you to design your own circuits.

Start

The car park near the surgery and tennis courts on the road out of Beckford towards Overbury

P As above

Distance and grade

7 and 10 miles (two loops, total 17 miles)

Moderate/strenuous

Terrain

Two steady 750-foot climbs from the southern side of the hill. May be muddy in the woods after rain. In general, broad, well-defined tracks

Nearest railway

Evesham, 6 miles from Ashton under Hill

Refreshments

Star Inn ●, **Ashton under Hill**
Beckford Inn ●, Coffee Shop, **Beckford**
Yew Tree PH, **Conderton**
Crown Inn ●, **Kemerton**

Beckford   Conderton Hill   Great Hill   Ashton under Hill   Beckford

Places of interest

Bredon Hill villages

The picturesque villages of Ashton under Hill, Beckford, Conderton, Overbury and Kemerton lie on this route. There is a lovely mixture of Cotswold stone and black and white timbered buildings.

Bredon Hill Fort 23

Bredon Hill is almost 1000 feet high and affords superb views over to Wales, the Vale of Evesham, the Rivers Severn and Avon, and to the Cotswolds. The Iron Age hill fort has two ramparts and was the scene of a savage battle at about the time of Christ, probably against the Belgic invaders; the hacked remains of 50 men were found near the entrance.

Off-road riding tips

- Padded shorts and gloves make off-road riding more comfortable

- If there is any chance of rain take something waterproof. Never underestimate the effects of wind-chill when you are wet, even in summer

- In wet and cold conditions keep a layer of warm clothes next to the skin – thermal underwear or wool

- Carry a water bottle in the bottle carrier and keep it filled, particularly on hot days

Overbury

Banbury Stone

Lower Westmancote

Kemerton

Loop 1

1 From the car park go back towards Beckford. At X-roads L on Court Farm Lane

2 At the farm follow the track between buildings, then R just past a stone barn with green doors up a broad stony track

3 Steep 450-foot climb to the edge of the wood. At X-roads at the start of the enclosed wooded section SA

4 At the end of the wood leave the broad, well-made track and turn L, following the edge of the wood along the field edge

5 Go through gate and head for a point just to the right of the radio masts, crossing the grassy field diagonally R uphill

6 Through field to a ruin and bear L on a more obvious track alongside the wall

7 Through gate and at T-j with main track R

8 Through gates to the edge of the wood. Turn R on major track, leaving the wood to your left

9 Follow the main ridge track past the end of the wood with a wall, fence then wall again to the left

10 Ignore two gates to the left with Wychavon Way signs. Go round two RH bends at the edge of field then at a tall wooden bridleway signpost L downhill through field gate

11 At a T-j of tracks bear L following blue arrow on less steep track towards gate

12 Follow instructions carefully! Through gate and after 100 yards bear R downhill on a faint grassy track before a line of trees in the field, bearing away from the more obvious track that goes straight ahead

13 Down through grass to a gate that leads onto a sunken track to your right

14 Follow the track downhill, passing a farm on your right into Ashton under Hill

15 At the end of Cottons Lane, at T-j with road in Ashton R following signs for Beckford and Overbury

16 At T-j in Beckford R 'Overbury' to return to start

Loop 2

17 From Beckford, follow road through Conderton into Overbury. Opposite the black and white timbered village store and Post Office turn R

18 After ½ mile, shortly after a raised grass verge on your left, L onto lane 'Private road, No unauthorised vehicles', 'Public Bridleway'

19 Steep climb on tarmac to a farm at the top

20 With the house ahead, bear R through gate into field

21 Continue in same direction through second gate and over brow of hill. At X-roads of tracks at edge of wood L

22 At end of the wood, SA through gate and follow fence on left. At the next gate follow wall then obvious track straight towards the tower

23 From the tower follow the wall into the wood on the main track

24 At the end of the wood sharply L, following signs, on grassy track down along field edge

25 At end of field L again on stony track. Follow this downhill to tarmac.

26 Ignore turnings to the right. At T-j with main road L 'Kemerton, Beckford, Overbury' to return to the start

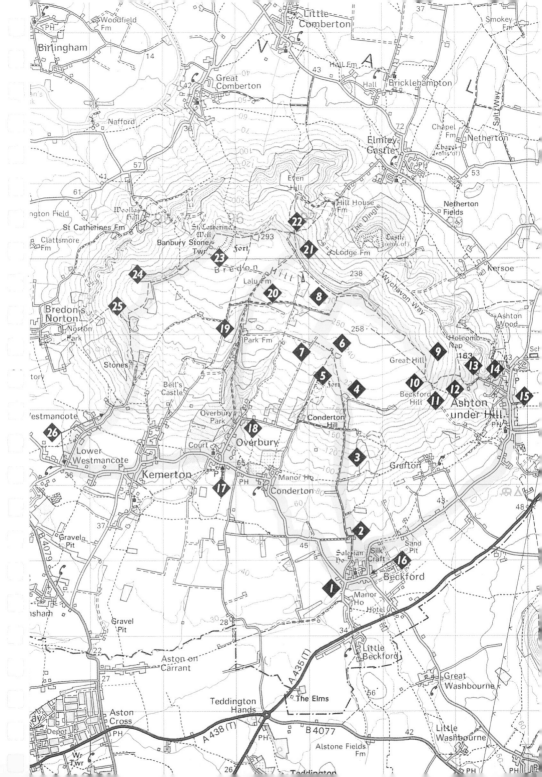

From Stanton up the Cotswold escarpment to Snowshill

The two beautiful Cotswold villages of Stanton and Snowshill are linked via a stiff climb and a thrilling descent to form an enormously satisfying loop. There are some excellent quality off-road tracks and you can reward your efforts with some refreshment in the highly recommended Mount Inn PH in Stanton.

Refreshments

Mount Inn PH ●●, **Stanton**
Snowshill Arms PH ●, **Snowshill**

Start

Car park in Stanton off the B4632 (was the A46) Winchcombe–Broadway road

P As above

Distance and grade

13 miles
///// Moderate

Terrain

A long steep climb of 600 feet from Buckland to Snowshill (Snozzle) and a shorter, more gentle 230 feet from near Taddington onto Shenberrow Hill. An exciting descent back down into Stanton

Nearest railway

Moreton-in-Marsh, 6 miles east of Snowshill

Stanton   Buckland   Snowshill

Stanton 1

A charming village with houses of warm honey-coloured stone restored by Sir Phillip Stott, the architect, who lived at Stanton House the Jacobean manor house from 1906-37.

Snowshill 7

A charming unspoilt village with a striking church and a row of much photographed cottages. The

manor house at Snowshill, a National Trust property, stands in an ancient estate owned by Hailes Abbey from 821 until 1539. It is a Tudor house with a 17th-century facade. The last owner, Charles Paget Wade, made a large collection of craftsmanship

▲ The bridleway between Snowshill and Hornsleasow Farm

that includes musical instruments, Japanese armour, clocks, toys, bicycles, weavers' and spinners' tools and is contained in the 21 rooms of the manor.

1 Turn L out of car park to join the B4632

2 Turn R on main road for 1¼ miles

3 Ignore signs for Laverton. Turn R at sign for 'Buckland ¼', no through road

4 Pass church and follow road through village as it turns from tarmac to track

5 At a junction of tracks next to a breeze-block-and-wood barn go SA up a stony track. The track improves shortly, views open up and the route contours the valley

6 At T-j by a triangle of grass L towards Snowshill. At next T-j L again into Snowshill

7 Go past pub and manor house, then sharply R, almost back on yourself 'Chipping Campden 5, Bourton-on-the-Water 10¼'

8 SA through two X-roads, following signs for Bourton-on-the-Water

9 On sharp RH bend with road coming in from the left go SA through gate onto a bridleway towards a wood (this section may be muddy after rain). Continue in same direction along LH edge of woodland then across field

10 At T-j with road R

11 At T-j with proper road, where there is a sign for Hornsleaslow Farm and Snowshill Hill, turn R

12 At T-j after 1½ miles SA onto track 'Unsuitable for motors'

13 At X-roads SA 'Stanway, Tewkesbury'

14 As road swings sharp left turn R 'Unsuitable for motors'

15 After less than ½ mile, as road bears round to the right, bear L through metal gates uphill onto track (blue arrow)

16 As broad track goes sharply left go SA through small metal gate (blue arrow)

17 Through several gates. At T-j with tarmac L. Ignore turnings to left and right. Follow this wonderful track downhill back into Stanton

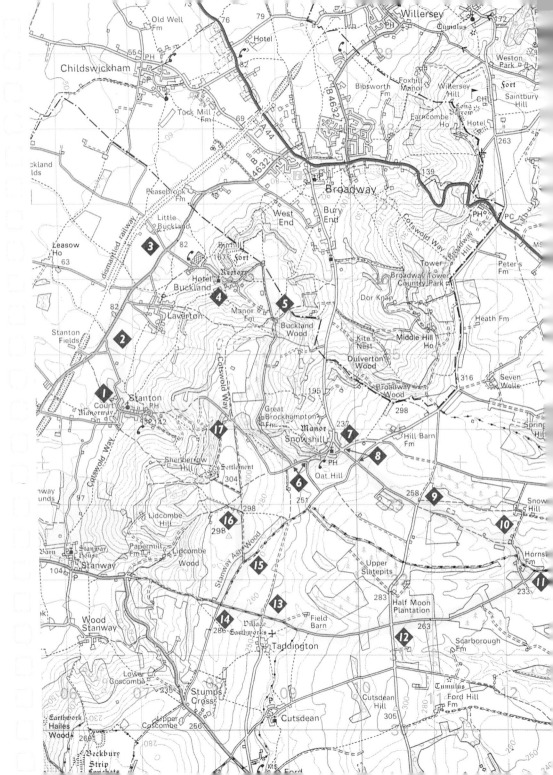

From Winchcombe to Cleeve Hill, the highest point on the Cotswolds

It is hard to think of the Cotswolds as bleak, but this ride to the highest point at the masts on Cleeve Hill does at times give that impression. However, views soon open up as you approach the edge of the escarpment, with Cheltenham spread out before you and the Vale of Gloucester stretching away to the west and north. Dodge the golfballs as you creep around the edge of the course then, having crossed the B4632, drop to the lowlands near Stanley Pontlarge to appreciate the escarpment from beneath. Gather your strength for the ascent of Stanley Mount and the fast descent back into Winchcombe.

Start

Tourist Information Centre, Winchcombe

[P] Long-stay car park on Back Lane off the Tewkesbury Road out of town

Distance and grade

15 miles

Strenuous

Terrain

A steep road climb of 650 feet from Winchcombe, fairly flat on top, then a long, bumpy descent from Nottingham Hill to Gotherington, a second climb to Dixton Hill and the final ascent up and over Stanley Mount to Winchcombe

Nearest railway

Cheltenham, 5 miles from the route at the radio masts

Refreshments

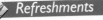

Plenty of choice in **Winchcombe**
Golf Clubhouse on **Cleeve Hill**
Shutter Inn, **Gotherington**
(1 mile off the route)
Royal Oak PH ♥♥, **Gretton**
(1 mile off the route)

Winchcombe

Wontley Farm

Cleeve Hill

Belas Knap Long Barrow 4

A 4000-year-old burial chamber in superb condition opened in 1863 to reveal 38 skeletons. At a height of nearly 1000 feet it is an excellent viewpoint.

Cleeve Cloud 9

Another superb viewpoint, Cleeve Cloud is an Iron Age camp with double ramparts and the 100-foot diameter circular earthwork called 'The Ring'.

▲ *A view from Nottingham Hill*

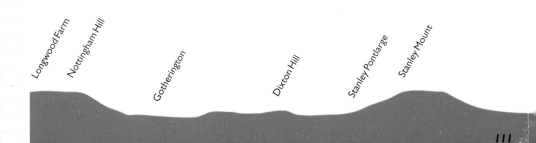

1 With your back to the Tourist Information Centre R out of town on the B4632 Cheltenham Road towards the White Hart Inn

2 Just past a row of pine trees, opposite Winchcombe Hospital L 'Brockhampton 4, Andoversford 6' and after 80 yards L onto Corndean Lane

3 Climb steeply. After 1¼ miles, on sharp LH bend bear R (in effect SA) 'Corndean Lane, West Downs'

4 After 150 yards bear L uphill 'Hillbarn Farm'

5 Past Hillbarn Farm, at X-roads of tracks at deserted Wontley Farm SA

6 Just before rejoining tarmac at Cleeve Hill Common Regulations sign R through gate 'Gallops' and head for masts

7 Go past masts and follow stone wall/fence on your left in the same direction as the views open up

8 At a fork of tracks, with a large yellow stone to the left and a metal bench up to the right, take L fork, taking as your bearing the cluster of red-brick buildings down on the plain

9 At tarmac near a small group of houses R. The track becomes rough again. Follow upper or lower track; they join up

10 Pass a cattle grid on your left and stay on the broad track above several groups of houses. After short steep climb the golf course starts on your right

11 At the clubhouse L over cattle grid onto tarmac. At X-roads with the B4632 SA '25% gradient'

12 As road bears L downhill SA onto track and through metal gate 'Public Path'

13 At the end of the main track, where a signpost gives you four options, bear L through the gate on the main track 'Gotherington 1 mile'

14 Aim to the right of the two round metal storage bins to go through metal gate with blue arrow

15 Follow bumpy track downhill past farm to tarmac. At T-j with road at the end of Manor Lane turn R (in winter or after rain follow road for 2½ miles. Rejoin at instruction 20)

16 After 100 yards 1st track L by house 'Bridleway'. Follow edge of fields (may be muddy in winter or after rain)

17 At farm do not go on obvious track to your left, but follow field edge, keeping farm buildings and farm itself to your left and joining a better uphill track near the house

18 After short, steep climb, broad track turns R to contour along hillside through fields, heading towards farm (may be muddy, particularly near one gate)

19 At road L then R by triangle of grass and oak tree onto no through road 'Dixton Manor'

20 Pass manor house. As drive bears R go SA through gate. SA through fields to rejoin road under powerlines at a bend in the road. Bear L

21 After ¾ mile, at top of small hill by post box R onto no through road 'Stanley Pontlarge'

22 Through farm. Steeply uphill on stony track to the top. At the top leave broad stony track and turn L uphill onto broad grassy track alongside line of trees

23 Carry on climbing SA onto narrow track between scrubby woodland

24 Through gate into field and follow RH field edge, bearing away from woodland to the left. This soon becomes a good broad track

25 At farm buildings bear L. Track turns to tarmac and descends steeply

26 At T-j with road L. After 100 yards at next T-j R. At T-j with main road L into Winchcombe

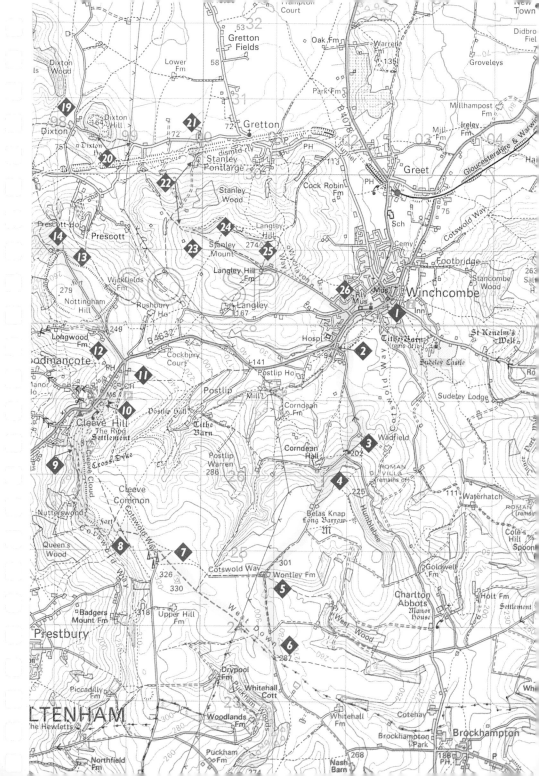

Through the northern Cotswolds on broad tracks

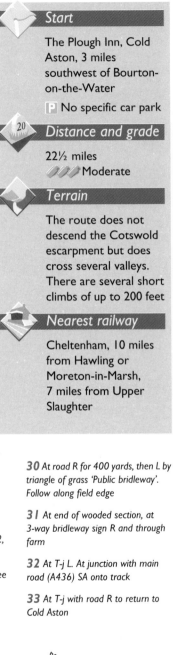

Start

The Plough Inn, Cold Aston, 3 miles southwest of Bourton-on-the-Water

P No specific car park

Distance and grade

22½ miles

Moderate

Terrain

The route does not descend the Cotswold escarpment but does cross several valleys. There are several short climbs of up to 200 feet

Nearest railway

Cheltenham, 10 miles from Hawling or Moreton-in-Marsh, 7 miles from Upper Slaughter

*F*alling within a circle of well-known places such as Stow-on-the-Wold, Bourton-on-the-Water, Cheltenham, Winchcombe and Moreton-in-Marsh, this ride nevertheless has a feel of being almost entirely off the beaten track (the one exception being Upper Slaughter). The ride is largely on broad stony all-year-round tracks. Where this is not the case, on the western side of the route, there is an on-road alternative on quiet lanes if you are undertaking the ride in winter, or after wet weather, or simply want to avoid the rougher, more overgrown sections.

1 With your back to the pub, turn L towards Notgrove. Shortly after passing the school on your right next L 'Unsuitable for motors'

2 After 2½ miles, at large sycamore tree by farmhouse fork R. At T-j with road after 50 yards R then L onto stony track immediately after barn with 'Grendon' sign

➡ page 117

23 At road L. At X-roads SA (NS). If you want a refreshment stop, go L following signs for Cotswold Farm Park

24 Soon after entering wood R 'Eyford Hill Farm' (blue arrow)

25 After 2 miles, at road L. At bottom of hill, just past house on left, R on 'Warden's Way'

26 At T-j with road by large sycamore tree R towards telephone box. Bear R through car parking area and R on road

27 At T-j L 'Lower Slaughter 1, Bourton-on-the-Water 2½'

28 On sharp LH bend, bear R (in effect SA) 'Bourton-on-the-Water 2, The Rissingtons'

29 After ½ mile, shortly after three stone barns on the left, opposite turning to left with white road markings R uphill on stony track

30 At road R for 400 yards, then L by triangle of grass 'Public bridleway'. Follow along field edge

31 At end of wooded section, at 3-way bridleway sign R and through farm

32 At T-j L. At junction with main road (A436) SA onto track

33 At T-j with road R to return to Cold Aston

Cold Aston   Turkdean   Hazleton   Salperton   Hawling

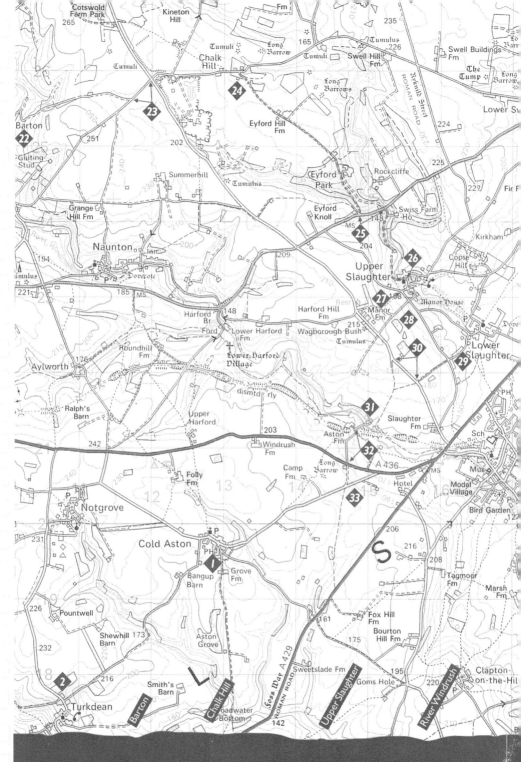

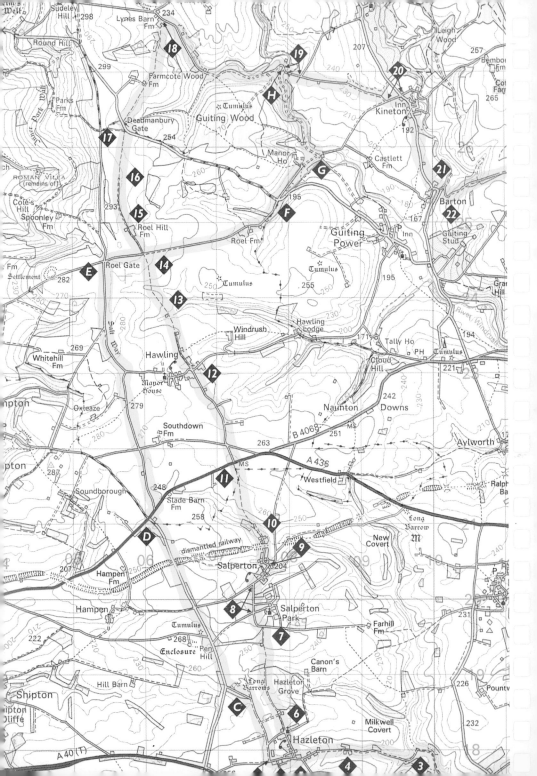

3 At bottom of valley, as main track ends at 2nd red gate, turn L through a grey gate towards plantation

4 Emerge past farm onto tarmac

5 1st road R 'St Andrew's Church'. At X-roads by triangle of grass and lime trees SA onto broad stony track

(Between instruction 5 and 19 the route occasionally crosses open fields that may be rough going in winter or after rain or may be overgrown in summer. For road alternative, on quiet lanes, avoiding sections which may be muddy, rutted, or overgrown see panel)

6 Past barn along LH edge of wood, following blue arrows. Continue in same direction into 2nd field with wood now to the left

7 At green gate at end of wood L

8 At X-roads SA 'Salperton'. At T-j by large crucifix R 'Bourton-on-the-Water 6¾, Stow-on- the-Wold 9'

9 At the bottom of the hill 1st L on no through road

10 Through green gate. At fork of tracks R uphill. Diagonally L uphill across next field to gates in far LH corner. Exit via RH of two gates into field ahead (blue arrow). Likely to be bumpy

11 At junction with main road (A436) SA 'Hawling 1¼, Winchcombe 6'

12 In Hawling, just past turning on right to Guiting Power and Naunton, on sharp LH bend bear R (in effect SA) downhill on no through road

---

Hazleton to Guiting Wood on-road alternative

A At instruction 5 **do not** turn R towards St Andrew's Church but go SA 'Northleach, Cheltenham'

B At end of village R 'Salperton 2¼, Winchcombe 9'

C At T-j R 'Salperton 1¼, Winchcombe 8'

D At T-j with A436 R 'Stow', then 1st L 'Hawling 2, Winchcombe'

E Follow signs for Winchcombe for 2½ miles. At X-roads R 'Guiting Power 3'

F At X-roads SA 'Kineton', 'Ford', 'Gates'

G 400 yards after 1st gate, before 2nd gate, by large horse- chestnut tree L 'Unsuitable for motors'

H Through gate. After 1 mile at T-j R. Rejoin main route at instruction 19 'climb steep hill'

---

13 Good track becomes overgrown but mainly rideable along the edge of several fields

14 Emerge at road. SA 'Roel Hill Farm'

15 Through farm and green gate and onto straight broad track

16 As track bears L go SA through wooden gate along field edge

17 Emerge at road. Turn L then R at the bottom of the dip just past a sign for 'Warden's Way' on a small easily missed track

18 Follow along field edge, past a disused house (keep this to your left), continue in same direction. At T-j with road R

19 After 1½ miles, at bottom of hill fork L and climb steep hill. At top of hill, on sharp LH bend SA uphill on stony track. (Look out for the large stone frog!)

20 At road L (NS). At T-j R 'Kineton, Guiting Power 2'

21 At bottom of hill, just after crossing stream, on sharp RH bend L through gate and uphill on stony track. After 70 yards sharply R

22 After 150 yards at green metal gate L following blue arrow

← **page 114**

Places of interest

The Slaughters 26-29

The villages of Lower and Upper Slaughter are linked by the River Eye. In Lower Slaughter the stream flows through the centre of the village alongside rows of cottages and is straddled by little footbridges of ancient weathered stone. On the western edge of the village stands the much painted 19th-century red-brick corn mill. Upper Slaughter lies a mile away on a hill above the stream, the site of a Bronze Age burial ground. To the east of the church is the castle mound where the Norman castle, a wooden building with stone walls, once dominated the village.

Refreshments

Halfway House ♥♥, **Kineton**
Tea and coffee (in the summer) at the **Cotswold Farm Park** (just off the route)
Plough PH ♥♥, **Cold Aston**
Plenty of choice in **Bourton-on-the-Water** (just off the route)

From Birdlip in and out of the Golden Valley to Woodmancote

*T*his part of the Cotswolds seems to be blessed with myriad short and longer sections of off-road tracks linked by quiet lanes. This ride can easily be linked to either or both of the rides that start from Bisley and Painswick. Starting from Birdlip, you drop gently over 3 miles through woodland before climbing out of the valley to Caudle Green. The upper Frome that has carved the Stroud Valley further south and east, is crossed between Caudle Green and Winstone.

Passing through the quiet hamlets of the Duntisbournes, the route crosses the A417 onto a track leading to the lovely houses of Woodmancote. The return half of the route is a similar mix of disused roads, tracks, bridleways and quiet lanes in and out of wooded valleys back to Birdlip.

Refreshments

Royal George PH, **Birdlip**

Start

Birdlip Stores, Birdlip

P Plenty of parking along the no through road 200 yards east of the shop, just off the road to Brimpsfield and Caudle Green on a sharp RH bend

Distance and grade

17 miles
Moderate

Terrain

The ride starts with a gentle 330-foot descent towards Miserden, climbs hills either side of Caudle Green (150 feet and 230 feet) to Winstone, crosses a couple of small valleys at Duntisbourne and Woodmancote and ends with a 300-foot climb to return to Birdlip

Nearest railway

Gloucester or Cheltenham 7 miles, Kemble 8 miles from the southern half of the route

Birdlip

Climperwell Farm

Caudle Green

Duntisbourne Abbots

Middle Duntisbourne

- Keep some spare dry clothes and shoes in the car to change into and carry some bin liners in the car to put dirty, wet clothes in

- Keep other possessions dry in very wet weather by carrying them in two sets of plastic bags

- Lower your saddle when going down steep off-road sections, keep the pedals level, stand up out of the saddle to let your legs absorb the bumps and keep your weight over the rear wheel

- Alter your starting point to take account of the wind direction so that you are not cycling back into the wind when you are tired

- Drink before you get thirsty and eat before you get hungry. Regular small amounts are better than a big lunch

▲ *A view from Birdlip Hill*

Woodmancote   Winstone   Brimpsfield

1 With your back to the stores R out of the village on the road towards Brimpsfield 'Brimpsfield ½, Caudle Green 3'

2 1st R 'Caudle Green'. Go round sharp LH bend. Just past Blacklains Farm on your left R on broad track along field edge 'Bridleway'

3 With hedge on your right follow track as it bears R around 2nd field. Just past post with two blue arrows L alongside wall towards the wood to your left

4 At corner of field where track turns sharply right uphill, bear L (in effect SA) along edge of wood 'Dogs on leads'

5 Follow rough grassy track downhill to the road.

6 At road SA onto track 'Strictly Private, No parking', 'Bridleway'

7 Follow main (lower) track marked with blue arrows (may be rutted or muddy)

8 At a fork in the tracks, with a tree ahead marked with two blue arrows, take the more distinct LH upper track to a gate, then follow the blue arrow sharply R

9 Track improves. Keep following stream downhill until reaching a small pond on your right. Do not cross stream, bear left on less major track (may be muddy)

10 Continue uphill (track improves then deteriorates) until gradient flattens at far end of wood with a stone wall to your right. Turn L along field edge (blue arrow)

11 At top of field, following field edge, R alongside stone wall

12 At gate at corner of field by white bridleway post, exit onto road, turn R

13 Through Caudle Green down steep hill. At T-j at bottom of hill, R 'Winstone 1½, Miserden 3½'

14 At T-j by 'Miserden Park Farms', R

15 After 300 yards 1st L 'Duntisbourne Abbotts, Unsuitable for motors'

16 At T-j by triangle of grass R 'Duntisbourne Leer ¾, Sapperton 4', then immediately L 'Duntisbourne Leer, Middle Duntisbourne'

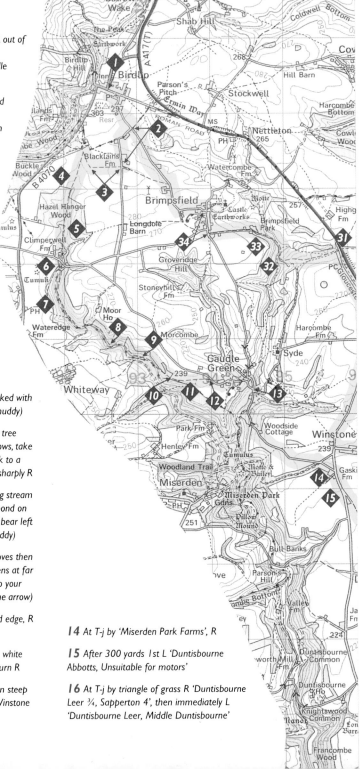

17 At T-j L then R following signs for Middle Duntisbourne and Daglingworth

18 At triangle of grass by sign for Middle Duntisbourne L 'Ford, B&B'

19 At T-j with A417 L then R 'Dartley Farm'. **Take care crossing this road**

20 At X-roads of tracks R towards stony track with grass growing in the middle

21 Follow this main track down, then up onto tarmac drive. Go up past houses to road

22 At road L 'Rapsgate 1½, Colesbourne 2½' (the sign is on your right)

23 2nd L opposite barn with green door, past house

24 Follow broad stone track through small wood, bearing L alongside stone wall

25 By metal barns with 'Moorwood Estate' signs go SA through gate into field

26 Downhill through field on obvious track. Exit field via gate, bearing R towards stone barns. Go past the main house onto tarmac and bear L at fork of tarmac tracks

27 At road L steeply down then uphill

28 At X-roads with A417 SA 'Miserden 3½' (**take care** – busy road)

29 At end of Winstone village, on sharp LH bend, by a sign for Jackbarrow Road R onto track

30 At X-roads with road SA

31 At T-j with A417 L through lay-by, then at the end of the lay-by L by large green metal box through gate into field 'Bridleway'

32 Follow along LH field edge through three fields. At start of the woodland R onto grassy track steeply downhill to gate

33 At pond fork L uphill past big house onto tarmac

34 At road R, then after 400 yards, just after phone box, L 'Birdlip'

Woodland tracks and panoramic viewpoints near Painswick

When you look at the area around Painswick on an Ordnance Survey map there are so many hills, valleys, lanes, tracks, woods and farms packed together in such a small space that it would be easy to despair of ever finding a continuous route for mountain biking. However, this ride provides just that, although it takes a very circuitous line to link together some very fine stretches of bridleway and track with some magnificent viewpoints from Painswick Golf Course and Haresfield Hill. Route-finding in the woods may be a little tricky, but blue arrows indicating bridlepaths have been liberally painted on trees. If in doubt, consult the map.

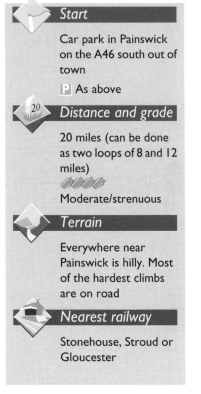

Start

Car park in Painswick on the A46 south out of town

P As above

Distance and grade

20 miles (can be done as two loops of 8 and 12 miles)

Moderate/strenuous

Terrain

Everywhere near Painswick is hilly. Most of the hardest climbs are on road

Nearest railway

Stonehouse, Stroud or Gloucester

Off-road riding tips

● After fixing a puncture, check the inside of the tyre for embedded thorns before replacing the inner tube. A screwdriver is useful for winkling out difficult thorns

● Anticipate hills by changing into the right gear before it gets tough

● If there is an easier gear when struggling up a hill use it, and let the bike do the work not your knee joints

Painswick   Edge   Haresfield Hill   Painswick Valley   Wick Street

Painswick 1

Painswick is known locally as the 'Queen of the Cotswolds' and the churchyard is known for its legendary 99 yew trees, planted in the 18th century with the tradition that the hundredth one will never grow. The village stocks are situated in St Marys Street. They are known as spectacle stocks from their shape and are one of only two such specimens in existence.

▲ *Inscription by the well at Edge*

Painswick Rococo Garden 32

The Painswick garden is the only complete survivor from the Rococo period that occurred during the transition from the formal style of the 17th century to the natural flowing shapes of the 18th century. The six-acre garden set in a Cotswold combe combines formal vistas, charming contemporary structures and winding woodland walks.

Refreshments

*Foston Ash PH ❧, **Whiteway***
*Butchers Arms PH ❧ ❧, **Sheepscombe***
(steep climb after pub!)
Royal Oak PH ❧ ❧, plenty of choice in
Painswick

Down Hill

Down Barn Farm

Sheepscombe

A46

Painswick Hill

1 From the car park go uphill towards town taking 1st L on Edge Road opposite the timbered lodge gate to the church yard

2 Down and up steeply. On LH bend by a grass triangle R

3 At 2nd triangle of grass bear R towards farm, then after 50 yards L at fork (horse sign) up a stony, muddy track, which becomes a firm grassy track

4 At T-j with tarmac L, then at next T-j L again 'Edge'

5 At T-j with A4173 L 'Edge, Stroud 3½', then 1st R 'Whitehill 2, Randwick 2½'

6 Ignore 1st right to Harescombe, take next R after row of cottages on to no through road 'Stockend'

7 At fork of tracks bear L uphill

8 At T-j with road R downhill. Don't let yourself go completely! 1st track L 'Haresfield Beacon 1.5 kilometres, Cotswold Way'. Some wooden steps. Show consideration to other users of the track

9 At T-j with road by the farm L very steeply uphill. After 1 mile detour via NT Shortwood Car Park to the viewpoint for fine views into the Severn Vale and across into Wales.

10 At T-j R 'Whiteshill ¾, Randwick 1½'

11 After ½ mile, just **before** a turning to the right to Randwick L by letter box by Stoneridge Farm .

12 Through gate into field, following edge of wood on your right as it bends away downhill to the left. Through a gateway down towards houses

13 Exit via gate on to tarmac. At minor X-roads SA. **Descend with care** to A46. R then 1st L 'Wick Street 1'

14 Descend then climb. At T-j L (NS)

15 Ignore 1st left (Pincot Lane) by triangle of grass. At 2nd triangle of grass follow road uphill round sharp RH bend and immediately R on stony track. Shortly fork R

16 Climb steeply to top. At junction of tracks sharp L through gate into grassy field. The track soon improves and enters wood. Follow track to road

17 Here you may turn L then L to return to Painswick. To continue route turn sharply R back on yourself onto B4070. After ½ mile, after sign for Slad L steeply downhill on track following telegraph poles. This section is technical. Lower your saddle and keep your weight over the back wheel

18 At road L. Follow to the end. At fork by sign 'Last turning point' bear L

19 Follow broad main track gently uphill for 1½ miles to T-j by car breakers. Turn L, then at road R for almost 2 miles

20 400 yards after Foston Ash PH L on drive between two houses (the RH one is Ebworth House Farm)

21 Go through two gates. Superb descent on main track, marked with blue arrows. After pond and a short climb, on a sweeping LH bend bear L away from main track, which leads to black corrugated shed

22 At X-roads SA towards house. Descend to Butchers Arms PH

23 Immediately after PH sharply uphill. This section will require some pushing, forking L in field and following blue arrows in the woodland. At T-j at top of steep section bear L then shortly fork R uphill alongside wall at RH edge of woodland ('No unauthorised entry' sign to the left)

24 Follow instructions carefully. At substantial clearing in the wood, where 4 tracks join, with a 4-way blue bridleway sign on an ivy-clad beech tree to your left bear L, passing the sign

25 Track becomes narrower and muddier as it descends towards Brook Farm Trout Fishery. Past pond, down and up steeply onto tarmac

26 Immediately after houses L to descend to the road near Cranham School

27 At road L then 1st R down then up to the A46

28 To minimize time on busy main road, if you can see and hear the A46, bear L on track to join it further left (south). If this sounds complicated, at T-j with A46 L

29 At Royal William PH R and follow tarmac to end. Where track forks, bear R past car park on obvious track, then head for trig point

30 From trig point follow obvious track, bearing slightly R along wood edge

31 At road SA on (signed) bridleway on raised grass embankment into wood, following blue arrows

32 At road L onto B4073, then at T-j with A46 R to return to start

East from Bisley on bridleways and disused roads in the Cotswolds

A delightful ride from the lovely village of Bisley, with its two pubs, a tea house and village stores. The ride makes use of many roads that have fallen into disrepair and are no longer suitable for cars but are ideal for mountain bikes. The route passes close to the beautiful manor house at Edgeworth and through the village of Duntisbourne Leer before returning west via more disused roads near Througham and Througham Slad to Bisley.

Refreshments

Bear Inn ♥♥, Stirrup Cup PH ♥, tea shop, **Bisley**

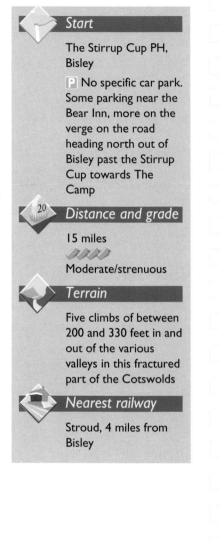

Start

The Stirrup Cup PH, Bisley

🅿 No specific car park. Some parking near the Bear Inn, more on the verge on the road heading north out of Bisley past the Stirrup Cup towards The Camp

Distance and grade

15 miles

Moderate/strenuous

Terrain

Five climbs of between 200 and 330 feet in and out of the various valleys in this fractured part of the Cotswolds

Nearest railway

Stroud, 4 miles from Bisley

Bisley · Battlescombe · Edgeworth · Middle Duntisbourne · Duntisbourne Leer

Off-road riding tips

● Let someone know where you are going, particularly if it is winter and you are going to a remote area

● If there is any possibility of cycling in twilight or darkness, take lights with you. As a precaution in winter, take a reflective belt and/or reflective strips for ankles and wrists – being visible is what matters most

● If your brake blocks look as though they are wearing thin, take a spare set with you. New brake blocks are much cheaper than new rims

● If there is a grating or crunching noise when you spin the wheels, pedals or cranks replace the bearings before they damage more expensive parts

● If some vegetation gets stuck in your derailleur, remove it straightaway before it does any damage

● The deepest part of a puddle on a farm track is usually where the vehicles wheels go, so try the higher ground in the middle

● Take a compass with you for crossing moorland or in poor visibility and know how to use it

● If using British Rail, always phone in advance to check what the regulations are for the service you wish to use and if a reservation is required

● Plan a group ride with the weakest person in mind

Duntisbourne Abbots   Lypiatt   The Camp   Througham   Battlescombe

1 With your back to the Stirrup Cup PH take the upper RH road 'Through traffic'

2 Shortly, at X-roads L 'Waterlane 1¼, Sapperton 3½'

3 After 300 yards, on sharp RH bend bear L (in effect SA) (sign for Waterlane and Sapperton to the right)

4 After 1½ miles , bear R at fork (do **not** go over cattle grid)

5 Steeply down, steeply up. Shortly after passing farm buildings/sawmill on the left, as track continues to climb uphill and left, leave main track and bear R by pine tree into wood

6 Follow main track out of wood along field edge to road. SA past West Lodge

7 SA through gate into field. Just past 1st telegraph pole bear L away from main descending track towards wooden fence and houses on your left

8 Through gate. At T-j R towards manor house 'Public Bridleway' then R again through gate just before main entrance (blue arrow) to go through gardens

9 At bottom of hill bear L towards stone pillars and gate

10 Uphill on track to road. At T-j R uphill

11 At X-roads R 'Sapperton 3, Stroud 10½'

12 Just before woodland and lodge for Cirencester Park L through gate along field edge on the north side of the wood

13 At road SA, bearing slightly R onto track

14 Follow track along field edgres, bearing L onto better track. At T-j with road L

15 After 1¼ miles R 'Duntisbourne Leer', then L 'Unsuitable for motor vehicles'

16 At T-j by telephone box L uphill, then at next T-j L 'Duntisbourne Leer ¾, Daglingworth 2¾'

17 Very shortly R 'Unsuitable for motor vehicles', then fork L onto stony track

18 At road SA

19 At T-j of tracks L, then R heading downhill towards house. At road L. Steep climb

20 At T-j R 'Birdlip 4½, Cheltenham 10½', then 1st L down track by stone wall 'Public path'

21 Follow this steeply down then up onto tarmac to road

22 At T-j L 'Bisley, Chalford'

23 1st L 'Througham'. 1st L again on entering wood, by stone walls, (NS)

24 Keep bearing R until road starts climbing. On sharp RH bend by a wooden gate. L onto stony track

25 At T-j with road by large house L downhill

26 At T-j with track by cattle grid R uphill, rejoining outward route

27 At T-j with road R 'Bisley'. At X-roads R 'The Camp, Stroud'

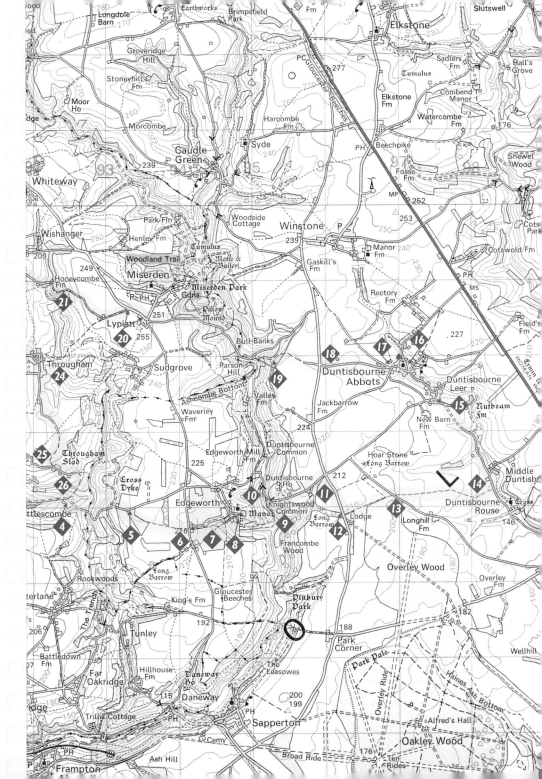

Ridges, railways and river banks in the beautiful Wye Valley

8

The Wye Valley between Chepstow and Monmouth is truly spectacular, particularly in the autumn when the colours of the leaves are changing. Car drivers can appreciate all its beauty driving along the A466. For cyclists, however, the road is a real nightmare, and this ride spends only a very short time on it near Tintern. Walkers have got Offa's Dyke Path and the Wye Valley Walk. So what is there for cyclists? As good fortune has it, parts of both the walks mentioned have bridlepath status and by linking them with part of a dismantled railway, forestry tracks and old green lanes you have two loops, one on either side of the river, which offer variety, challenge, good views and three excellent pubs.

Start

Brockweir Inn, Brockweir, just off the A466 Chepstow – Monmouth road.

P In the lay-by just beyond the Brockweir Inn

Distance and grade

8 and 14 miles (two loops, with two links of 1½ miles; total 25 miles

Moderate/Strenuous

Terrain

Two long climbs, one of 800 feet from Tintern up onto the Wye Valley Walk north of Cleddon, and one of 600 feet from Redbrook to Wyegate Green

Nearest railway

Chepstow, 6 miles south of Tintern

Brockweir   Tintern Parva   Cleddon   The Narth   Redbrook   Newland

Tintern Abbey /

Tintern Abbey is one of the finest ruins in the country; founded in 1131 the abbey owes much of its beauty to its peaceful setting in the Wye Valley. The ruins of the church date back to the 13th century and the remains of many domestic buildings have also survived, including the chapter house, sacristy, parlour, refectory and kitchen.

Refreshments

Brockweir Inn ✿ ✿, **Brockweir**
Ostrich PH ✿ ✿, **Newland**
Boat Inn ✿ ✿, **Redbrook**
Plenty of choice in **Tintern**

Old Station, Tintern /

The former railway station now houses a small exhibition telling the story of the Wye Valley railway.

▲ Tintern Abbey

1 With your back to the Brockweir Inn L over the bridge. At T-j with A466 L 'Chepstow'. Just past the Wye Valley Hotel R 'Catbrook 2'

2 Ignore turn to Catbrook. At T-j SA into Forestry Commission land 'Tintern, Whitestone'. After 20 yards SA and slightly L up narrower, steep rough track

3 Continue in the same direction as track broadens into forestry track (may be muddy). At road SA 'Pen-Y-Fan. Wye Valley Walk'

4 Follow signs for Wye Valley Walk along ridge until reaching a wooden gate across the track near a clearing. Turn L through a second gate (yellow arrow) to cross field. Through another gate onto a track/ driveway. Emerge at road. L then immediately R 'Manorside'

5 At T-j with road L. At T-j by triangle of grass R 'The Narth, Penalt'. Ignore turnings to right and left for 1½ miles. Shortly after passing a small red-brick house on your right, opposite a bridleway sign on your left turn R down Warrens Road

6 At T-j L then R by telephone box. Shortly after forestry starts on your right R through a wooden barrier for a mega descent

7 At T-j at the bottom L on the dismantled railway track to cross bridge over river at Redbrook

8 At the end of the bridge turn R. At the main road, **take care**. After 400 yards sharply L back on yourself onto Coach Road

9 Keep to the left, following signs for Glyn Farm, then Birt Cottage, leaving all the buildings you pass to your right

10 Emerge onto better track, which turns to tarmac near to the water treatment works. Follow the road as it bears right along the valley floor. At T-j with more major road, with Rose Cottage and Rookery Farm opposite, R for 50 yards then R again up track.

11 Climb steeply, then more gently to road. At T-j R. At the next group of buildings (Stowe Green Farm), after ½ mile R on no through road to some buildings at the end

12 At buildings R and follow Coxbury and Wyegate Lane all the way to Redbrook. Do not go through any gates

13 In Redbrook retrace outward route, crossing the railway bridge, re-joining the dismantled railway track and following this 2½ miles to a road

14 Follow road along the valley as far as Bigsweir Bridge. Cross the river on this bridge then R along Offa's Dyke Path, following **blue** arrow or signs for **horses** if the path divides to return to Brockweir

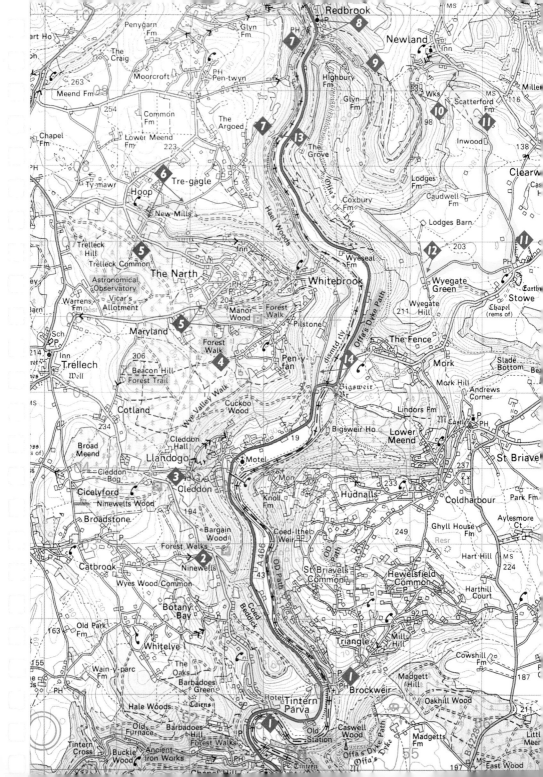

An introduction to the eastern side of the Forest of Dean

The Forest of Dean is a very special area for mountain biking. Run by the Forestry Commission it covers an area of 35 square miles and is criss-crossed with hundreds of miles of excellent quality tracks. There are three areas where cycling is **not** allowed: the Arboretum (fenced), the National Nature Reserve at Ladypark Wood (fenced) and Nagshead Nature Reserve (look out for 'No Cycling' signs). The Forest of Dean offers a tremendous variety of off-road cycling unmatched in almost all of southern England, where you can turn up without any fixed route and enjoy rides of different grades. The ride described here certainly does not claim to be definitive: more a taste of the eastern side of the forest with some fabulous views over the Severn and some great tracks through dense woodland.

You can obtain more details by contacting the following addresses: Forestry Commission, Crown Offices, Bank Street, Coleford, Gloucestershire, tel: 01594-33057 and the Forest of Dean Tourist Information Centre, Coleford, Gloucestershire, tel: 01594-36307

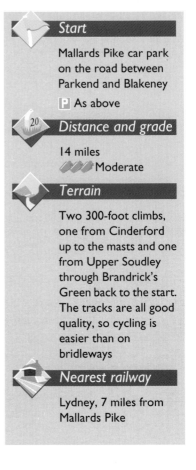

Start

Mallards Pike car park on the road between Parkend and Blakeney

P As above

Distance and grade

14 miles

Moderate

Terrain

Two 300-foot climbs, one from Cinderford up to the masts and one from Upper Soudley through Brandrick's Green back to the start. The tracks are all good quality, so cycling is easier than on bridleways

Nearest railway

Lydney, 7 miles from Mallards Pike

Mallards Pike

Bilson Green

Edge Hills

Places of interest

Dean Heritage Centre, Soudley 22
This is situated by the mill pond at Soudley
which lies in a beautiful wooded valley. It is a
museum of forest life with displays of
industrial history including the beam engine
and waterwheel; natural history exhibits; a
small-holding;
15-frame
observational
beehive; a
wood ants'
nest; charcoal
burning and
woodcraft
skills; nature
trails; craft
shop and
workshops;
café and
adventure
play area.

▲ *Mallards Pike Lake*

Refreshments

Plenty of choice in **Cinderford**
Littledean House Hotel, **Littledean**
Teas, snacks at Dean Heritage Centre, **Lower Soudley**
White Horse PH, **Upper Soudley**

Cinderford

Littledean

Dean Hill

Upper Soudley

1 From the car park head away from the road round the wooden barrier on track parallel with the lake (ie **not** alongside the lake itself). The lake is on your right

2 At the end of the first lake R on a broad track between the lakes

3 Follow this round a LH bend and climb gently for 1¼ miles following the telegraph poles

4 At T-j R through wooden gate. Follow this uphill as the track bears sharply L to join a more major track coming up from the right

5 The track climbs, descends over cobbles and climbs again, once more following the telegraph poles.

6 At T-j with B4226 L uphill past Forest of Dean sign then 1st R onto track after 300 yards opposite sign for 'Lightmoor Works' on your left

7 Follow in same direction until X-roads of tracks near to car-breakers. Go SA onto narrow track between wooden stakes and under pipe. At X-roads of major tracks, do not take the main track ahead but bear slightly R between wooden stakes onto narrower, gravel track in the pine wood

8 At X-roads of tracks with the lake ahead ('Forestry Commission, Private Fishing') R on broad track following telegraph poles

9 Bear L to join road by large red-brick/green-roof warehouses. Turn L

10 At T-j with main road (A4151), R then immediately L onto track

11 Follow this track uphill over discarded asphalt then over three X-roads (lift your bike over stiles if the gates are locked) towards masts

12 Opposite the fenced in compound around the masts, **before** reaching the white cottage, turn R then immediately fork R through wooden barrier onto broad track

13 Follow in the same direction gently downhill to the road

14 At road L past youth centre and 'Splinters'

15 Fabulous views open up. At Royal Foresters PH 2nd L on The Ruffit 'No cars except for access'

16 Steeply downhill to Littledean House Hotel. At T-j L on Broad Street

17 At roundabout R 'Littledean Hall, Newnham 2'

18 At crown of hill, as road starts to drop, by a triangle of grass R uphill 'No access to Forestry Commission picnic site'. Bear L at fork

19 At large triangle of grass R on stony track towards stone-built house with five windows, two chimneys and a porch

20 At X-roads of tracks ('No Entry' signs ahead) R downhill

21 Descend to car park and turn L through parking area towards barricade

22 At T-j with road R (**or** L to Dean Heritage Centre for tea stop)

23 Through Upper Soudley and past White Horse PH. At the end of the village, on sharp RH bend L 'Blackpool Bridge 1¼'

24 At top of small hill with no through road to left signposted 'Bradley Hill' turn R. Take the LH, lower track at the fork

25 Climb steeply on the main track to wonderful viewpoint over the forested valley by some outcrops of rock. Shortly, as track swings R uphill turn L

26 Track climbs then descends. At wide gravel area turn L sharply back on yourself. Just before the cattle grid and road, turn sharply R back to Mallards Pike Car Park

⚠ The Forest of Dean

The Forest of Dean is a working forest environment and the surfaces of the tracks through it are often liable to change. In addition, new tracks are built so that instructions are at times difficult to relate to what you may see before you. Remember that you are never more than two miles from a road anywhere in the forest so do not despair – you cannot get irretrievably lost!

10 A double loop in the southern Cotswolds near Hawkesbury Upton

A ride on the Cotswold escarpment along valleys and through woodland, passing many lovely Cotswold stone buildings. The ride starts at the high point with fabulous views out across the Vale of Severn. Over tracks and along field edges, the ride crosses the A46 after Bodkin Hazel Wood. Soon you have the unusual experience of crossing a landing strip – watch out for planes! The second loop descends through woodland, which is muddy after rain and in winter, down to Lower Kilcott before climbing again to Alderley. A final climb past Splatt's Barn will return you to the start.

Places of interest

Horton Court 3
A National Trust Cotswold manor house with a 12th-century Norman hall and Renaissance features. There is also a late Perpendicular ambulatory detached from the house.

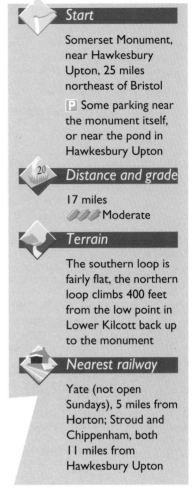

Start

Somerset Monument, near Hawkesbury Upton, 25 miles northeast of Bristol

P Some parking near the monument itself, or near the pond in Hawkesbury Upton

Distance and grade

17 miles
Moderate

Terrain

The southern loop is fairly flat, the northern loop climbs 400 feet from the low point in Lower Kilcott back up to the monument

Nearest railway

Yate (not open Sundays), 5 miles from Horton; Stroud and Chippenham, both 11 miles from Hawkesbury Upton

Highfield Farm

Widdenhill Farm

- If using a jet spray to clean your bike, do not aim the hose directly at the hubs or bottom bracket – clean these parts from above

- Lubricate your bike after washing it or after a very wet ride, paying particular attention to the chain

- Experiment with saddle height, forwards and backwards adjustment of saddle, tilt of saddle up or down and height of the handlebars (do not exceed maximum height) until you find your most comfortable riding position

- The same off-road route can take much longer after rain or in the winter when tracks are softer, so plan accordingly

- Good energy foods which don't take up much space are dates, figs, dried fruit and nuts

- If you come across a blocked right of way or one you feel is in a terrible state of repair report it to the Rights of Way Department at the County Council. The most effective means is to write a letter giving grid references

- When riding in a group ensure everyone has the equipment to mend a puncture (pump, tyre levers, puncture repair kit and/or spare inner tube). With four other tools: a reversible screwdriver, a small adjustable spanner, a set of appropriate allen keys and a chain link extractor you have all you need. All this fits in a small pouch, worn around your waist or attached under the saddle

Somerset Monument

Lower Kilcott

Alderley

Hillesley

1st Loop

1 With back to the monument L for 600 yards. At the village pond R 'Cotswold Way'

2 After 100 yards L 'Horton 3.5 kilometres'. Follow track for 1 mile (mud after rain) to road

3 At road R. Follow for 1 mile. At RH bend sharply L on broad track

4 Emerge at A46. **With great care**, R then L into wood, then immediately R

5 After 200 yards, at X-roads of tracks L through wooden gate to follow hedgerow

6 Follow main track across concrete farm track into next field. After 2nd stone wall L on to road

7 At road R for ½ mile. 10 yards before the lodge on your right turn R onto stone-based track through gate by cypress hedge. Follow track as it turns R towards grey corrugated iron shed

8 Between buildings, across landing strip and down into hollow. As track starts climbing, turn L along faint hedgerow opposite 3rd gate opening in stone wall on your right towards trees on horizon

9 At edge of the woodland R then L. At X-roads with major track in the strip of woodland SA onto narrow track

10 Follow this track round to the R and exit woodland via wooden gate into the field

11 You are aiming directly for the A46 along the LH edge of the stone wall. The farmer is obliged to re-establish the track after ploughing. If he has not please contact Gloucestershire Rights of Way Dept. At edge of wood by the road, follow the field round to the L for 10 yards looking out for opening through the trees on your right. Cross A46 (**take care**) onto road opposite

12 1st R up single track lane 'Hawkesbury Upton 2½'. At T-j L past Fox PH to start point

2nd Loop

13 From monument 300 yards downhill on main road. As road bears L at junction of bridleways 1st R 'Lower Kilcott 2 kilometres, Alderley 4 kilometres'

14 Through gate following blue arrow on well-defined track across field to wood

15 Through gate, take LH track, blue arrow. At times very muddy

16 Through metal gate at edge of wood. Follow blue arrow/white dot round edge of field. At T-j with track turn L through wooden gate

17 Fast descent to road. Turn L. After ¾ mile just before road starts to climb, R on track over bridge 'Cotswold Way'

18 After 100 yards at junction of bridleways L through gate with blue arrow and white dot

19 Follow track uphill through several gates to road. At road L downhill. Go through Hillesley, ignoring roads to right and left

20 Start to climb. As road bends L, opposite long metal gate on your right turn L up track

21 Through woodland, past Splatt Barn to rejoin outgoing route. L on road to monument

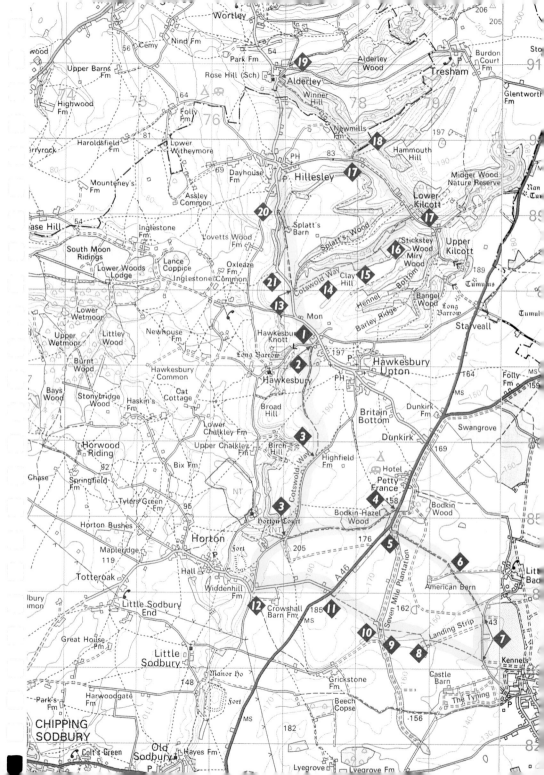

Cycle
TOURS

The Ordnance Survey Cycle Tours series

Around Birmingham
Avon, Somerset & Wiltshire
Berks, Bucks & Oxfordshire
Cornwall & Devon
Cumbria & the Lakes
Dorset, Hampshire & Isle of Wight
East Anglia – South
Gloucestershire and Hereford & Worcester
Kent, Surrey & Sussex
Southern Scotland

The whole series is available from all good bookshops or by mail order direct from the publisher. Payment can be made by credit card or cheque/postal order in the following ways

By phone

Phone through your order on our special *Credit Card Hotline* on *01933 414000*. Speak to our customer service team during office hours (9am to 5pm) or leave a message on the answer machine, quoting your full credit card number plus expiry date, your full name and address and reference T503N73C

By post

Simply fill out the order form opposite and send it to:
Cash Sales Department, Reed Book Services, PO Box 5, Rushden, Northants, NN10 6YX

Cycle TOURS

I wish to order the following titles

Title	Price	Quantity	Total
Around Birmingham ISBN 0 600 58623 5	£9.99		
Avon, Somerset & Wiltshire ISBN 0 600 58664 2	£9.99		
Berks, Bucks & Oxfordshire ISBN 0 600 58156 X	£9.99		
Cornwall & Devon ISBN 0 600 58124 1	£9.99		
Cumbria & the Lakes ISBN 0 600 58126 8	£9.99		
Dorset, Hampshire & Isle of Wight ISBN 0 600 58667 7	£9.99		
East Anglia – South ISBN 0 600 58125 X	£9.99		
Gloucestershire and Hereford & Worcester ISBN 0 600 58665 0	£9.99		
Kent, Surrey & Sussex ISBN 0 600 58666 9	£9.99		
Southern Scotland ISBN 0 600 58624 3	£9.99		

Postage and packing free　　　　　　　　　　　　　Grand total ☐

Name _____ (block capitals)

Address _____

_____ Postcode

I enclose a cheque/postal order for £ ☐ made payable to **Reed Book Services Ltd**

or please debit my ☐ Access ☐ Visa ☐ American Express ☐ Diners account

number ☐☐☐☐ ☐☐☐☐ ☐☐☐☐ ☐☐☐☐

by £ ☐ expiry date ☐☐ ☐☐ _____ Signature

• **Free postage and packing** • Whilst every effort is made to keep prices low, the publisher reserves the right to increase prices at short notice. • Your order will be despatched within 28 days, subject to availability
• Registered office: Michelin House, 81 Fulham Road, London SW3 6RB. Registered in England No 1974080